WILL DO MY BEST

O GOD AND MY

OBEY THE SCOUT

OTHER PEOPLE AT

KEEP MYSELF

NG, MENTALLY

RALLY STRAIGHT

To Ray

Our many thanks and best wishes
from the
Pony Express District

October 28-61

THE GOLDEN ANNIVERSARY

BOOK OF
SCOUTING

THE GOLDEN ANNIVERSARY

BOOK OF SCOUTING

by R. D. BEZUCHA
*assisted by the Staff of the National Council of
the* BOY SCOUTS OF AMERICA

Illustrated by NORMAN ROCKWELL
MEL CRAWFORD, JOHN LEONE, RAY JOHNSON

GOLDEN PRESS · NEW YORK

ACKNOWLEDGMENTS

The paintings by Norman Rockwell courtesy Brown & Bigelow, St. Paul, Minnesota.

The portrait of Lord Baden-Powell on page 10 courtesy the Boy Scouts Association, London, England.

The illustrations by Lord Baden-Powell on pages 11, 17–22, 40, 46, and 90 courtesy Lady Baden-Powell.

The drawings by Ernest Thompson Seton on page 26 are from *Two Little Savages* by Ernest Thompson Seton, published by Doubleday and Company.

The drawing by Daniel Carter Beard on page 27 is from *Buckskin Book for Buckskin Men and Boys* by Daniel Carter Beard, published by J. B. Lippincott Company.

The photograph of Rudyard Kipling on page 45 courtesy the Culver Service.

The photograph of Norman Rockwell on page 147 courtesy Mr. Rockwell and the Lincoln-Continental Division, Ford Motor Company.

The portrait of Dr. Schuck on page 163 is by Paul Trebilcock. The paintings on pages 63, 73, and 99 are by Lawrence Wilbur. The four paintings are used through the courtesy of the National Council of the Boy Scouts of America.

Certain illustrations on pages 38, 40–2, 63, 73, 89, 91, 99, 144–9, 154, 156–7, 159, and on the back cover and jacket are copyright by the Boy Scouts of America. The paintings by Norman Rockwell on the jacket, the cover, and pages 7, 37, 43, 52, 65, 85, 94, 114, 142, and 151 are copyright by Brown & Bigelow, St. Paul, Minn.

SECOND PRINTING

C O N T E N T S

INTRODUCTION 11

The Unknown Scout 13

The Baden-Powell Story 16

Early Days in America 24

Shaping the American Program 34

Cub Scouting 44

Boy Scouting 66

Scouting for Older Boys 90

Volunteer Leaders 115

Local Organization 121

National Organization 128

Scouting Marches On 136

The Goal Ahead 162

INDEX 164

BIBLIOGRAPHY 165

Scouting Is 50 Years Old

WHEN THE BOY SCOUT MOVEMENT came of age a number of years ago, the founder, Lord Baden-Powell of Gilwell, drew a sketch that showed how the "acorn" of the Scout idea which he planted on tiny Brownsea Island had grown into the "oak" of Scouting—spreading its branches around the world.

The mightiest branch of that Scouting "oak" is the Boy Scouts of America, with a membership today of more than five million boys and leaders.

The growth of the Boy Scouts of America from a struggling youth movement among many others in 1910, to its present pre-eminence in the youth field is a remarkable story. I am proud indeed to have been given the opportunity to tell that story in *The Golden Anniversary Book of Scouting*.

For the more than 28,000,000 former members of the Boy Scouts of America, the reading of this Golden Book will, I hope, bring back memories of happy days with the "old gang" in woods and fields. To the Scouts of today and tomorrow, the book should provide excitement and challenge. To the general public the book, I am sure, will be an eye opener to the scope and importance of the contribution of the Scout movement to the life of America.

It is because of this contribution that the Boy Scouts of America are respected and beloved by the country. Almost from the beginning the Scout movement in America was accepted as "a good thing." Fortunately, the Boy Scouts of America, through wise leadership, has successfully evaded the complacency, the "resting on the laurels" that often results from being considered "a good thing." It has constantly kept abreast with the currents in American life and for this reason is more dynamic today on its fiftieth anniversary than ever before in its history.

The Boy Scouts of America enters its second half-century with the promise of still further growth. This growth is one of the finest assurances that America has of a future citizenry that is "physically strong, mentally awake, and morally straight" — worthy of our country and fit to serve her.

R. D. BEZUCHA

LORD BADEN-POWELL OF GILWELL
Founder of the Boy Scout Movement
Painted by David Jagger 1929
A gift of the Scouts of the world to their Chief

The Unknown Scout

THE BRITISH CAPITAL lay in the grip of a dense "pea soup" fog. It had rolled in during the night and had enveloped the whole city in its smoky yellowness. The famous London buses crawled cautiously along but other traffic had come to an almost complete standstill. Street lamps had been lit before noon. They shone with a feeble glow that penetrated only a few feet into the murkiness.

A man walking slowly along the poorly lit street stopped under a lamp post and tried to orient himself. He had the feeling that he had gone astray but in what direction was he to turn?

A dark figure emerged from the gloom. A boy moved past the man—then turned and came back.

"Can I help you, sir?" the youngster asked.

"You certainly can," said the man. "I have a business appointment somewhere around here. I'll be much obliged if you'll tell me how to get there." There was no mistaking the man's nationality—he spoke with a decided American accent.

"If you'll give me the address I'll take you there."

As they reached the destination the American pulled a shilling from his pocket for a tip.

A GOOD TURN TO A STRANGER

"No thank you, sir," the boy said, "not for doing a good turn."

"And why not?" the American asked.

"Because I'm a Scout!"

"A Scout? And what does that mean?"

"Haven't you heard about Baden-Powell's Boy Scouts?"

The American had not. "Tell me about them," he said.

The boy told him what he could of himself and his brother Scouts and all the fun they were having in Scouting.

But the American wanted to know still more.

"I know where you can find out," said the boy. "Our headquarters is close by, in Victoria Street. The General may even be in the office today."

"The General?"

"Baden-Powell himself, sir."

"Fine," said the American. "Let me finish my errand. Then, if you have time, we'll go to your headquarters."

The boy waited, then showed the way to the Scout office—and disappeared before the American had a chance to learn his name. . . .

BOYCE MEETS BADEN-POWELL

At the Boy Scouts' headquarters, the American—51-year-old William D. Boyce, newspaper and magazine publisher from Chicago, Illinois—met the founder of the Boy Scout movement, the British military hero, Lieutenant-General Robert S. S. Baden-Powell, and learned about Scouting from the Chief Scout himself.

Boyce became tremendously impressed with the possibilities of the movement that Baden-Powell had started. Through his business enterprises, he had had many dealings with boys, but no experience with them had ever struck him as forcibly as his first encounter with a Boy Scout.

When he left for the United States a few days later, he carried with him a trunkful of Scout literature, uniforms, and insignia. The moment he arrived home, he took steps to introduce the Boy Scout idea to America. He counseled with his friend, Colin H. Livingstone, of Washington, D.C., and with other people in the country's capital, and with them established a new corporation.

The name: BOY SCOUTS OF AMERICA

The date: FEBRUARY 8, 1910

In this way, a good turn done to a stranger by an unknown English Scout brought Scouting to the United States.

Seventeen years after he had done his good turn, the boy who had wanted nothing for himself received the highest award the Boy Scouts of America has to offer—the Silver Buffalo presented for "distinguished service to boyhood."

The regular Silver Buffalo is a small replica of an American buffalo, suspended from a white-and-red ribbon around the recipient's neck. In the case of the Unknown Scout, his award took the shape of a large bronze cast of a buffalo mounted on a wooden pedestal, erected at the International Boy Scout Training Center at Gilwell Park, England.

The boy himself was not there for the ceremony—he was never found—but the Prince of Wales was there to receive the award in his behalf from the American ambassador, Alanson Bigelow Houghton. The Chief Scout, Baden-Powell, and other prominent men of Great Britain and the United States were present as a plaque with a simple but eloquent inscription was unveiled:

To the Unknown Scout Whose Faithfulness in the Performance of the 'Daily Good Turn' Brought the Scout Movement to the United States of America.

THE SILVER BUFFALO

The Baden-Powell Story

WHAT WAS IT that had caught the imagination of this unknown English boy to such an extent that he was able to interest a stranger from a far-off country?

It was the game of SCOUTING—given to him and his British brothers by the man who, out of his genius and love for boys, had founded the Boy Scout movement.

To understand Scouting and its successful spread around the world it is necessary to know this man: Lord Baden-Powell of Gilwell, British military hero, author, artist, Chief Scout of the World—known to Scouts everywhere as "B.-P."

THE BEGINNING OF THE STORY

Robert Stephenson Smyth Baden-Powell was born in London, England, February 22, 1857, the fifth son and eighth child of H. G. Baden-Powell and Henrietta Smyth. His father was a man of many talents—clergyman, naturalist, and professor at Oxford University. His mother was the daughter of the British admiral W. H. Smyth.

Robert never knew his father well. He died when the boy was three, leaving the mother with nine children. "How that wonderful woman managed to bring us all up," said Baden-Powell many years later, "I do not know and cannot understand. It was her influence that guided me through life. . . ."

At thirteen, young Robert entered Charterhouse School. He was not a particularly brilliant pupil—one of his school reports says: "In mathematics he appears to have lost interest in the study; during French he frequently seems to fall asleep." But he was one of the liveliest boys in the school and a good goal keeper on the soccer team.

Robert spent many of his happiest hours at Charterhouse in "The Copse," a stretch of woodland outside the school grounds which was out of bounds to the pupils. Here he taught himself to snare rabbits and to cook them over a fire so small that the smoke would not give him away to a prowling teacher. He also learned to use an axe, to follow the tracks of wild animals, and to study animals—abilities which would be of great use to him in later life.

During his school vacations he joined his four brothers in outdoor adventures—paddling up the Thames River to its source, hiking in Wales and Scotland, and boating along the English coast.

At the time of Baden-Powell's graduation from Charterhouse, the British Army announced an open examination for commissions as officers. Robert took the examination and of 700 candidates, finished second. Because of the urgent need for officers for overseas duty he received an immediate commission as sublieutenant. At the age of 19, B.-P. left England to join his regiment in India.

As a boy in England

As a man in Africa

"The Copse" at Charterhouse. Watercolor painted by Baden-Powell at the age of 17.

*From one of Baden-Powell's
Indian sketch books*

A YOUNG OFFICER
IN INDIA

In India, Baden-Powell threw himself whole-heartedly into soldiering. He was a quick learner and proved himself particularly good at scouting and surveying on expeditions into the wild northwestern part of the country.

Unlike most of the other British officers in India in those days, young Baden-Powell had little money of his own to add to his small military pay. Yet he was eager to take part in all the regimental sports in which the other officers indulged—especially polo and hunting. He soon found a way of earning the extra money he needed. Using his writing and sketching ability he started a series of articles for an English magazine, for which he was well paid. He also bought untrained horses, trained them in his sparetime and sold them to other officers at a profit.

He became so good at polo that he was placed on the regimental team, and so proficient at wild-boar hunting on horseback—"pig-sticking"—that he won the all-India trophy in this sport.

After eight years' service in India, Baden-Powell—now a captain—returned with his regiment to England. But on the way home, the ship was ordered to South Africa—there was trouble in the British colony of Bechuanaland. While his regiment remained in Port Natal, Baden-Powell was sent into the frontier region alone to survey the mountain passes in case the regiment had to move inland. After a journey of six hundred miles on horseback, his task was finished. The trouble simmered down without military action, and the regiment continued to England.

During the next two years—1885–86—Baden-Powell had the chance to travel on secret service missions into Germany and Russia with his younger brother Baden, also an officer in the British Army. Their work in Russia was particularly daring. They had been sent to investigate reports that the Russian Army had developed a new type of military balloon.

Wild boar hunting on horseback

A peculiar Englishman hunting butterflies in the Balkans

The two brothers found out all they wanted to know but were arrested before they could get away. They tricked their guards and got back to England with their information.

In 1887, Baden-Powell's uncle, General Sir Henry Smyth, was made commanding officer of British South Africa. He invited his nephew to join him as his aide. B.-P. jumped at the opportunity and immediately sailed for Cape Town. Soon after his arrival, one of the Zulu tribes to the north rose in rebellion against the British. Baden-Powell was appointed staff officer for the forces sent in to suppress the uprising. The rebellious Zulu chief, Dinizulu, quickly gave up the fight and order was restored.

After further successful action against the Zulus, Major Baden-Powell was assigned to the island of Malta as intelligence officer for the whole Mediterranean area. Here he had full scope for his abilities as a spy. He went on numerous missions into Austria, Italy, Albania, Turkey, and other countries of southern Europe. He learned to disguise himself in different ways—posing as an artist sketching mountain landscapes in the Alps where Austrian troops were holding maneuvers, or as a butterfly hunter among the fortifications of the Dalmatian coast. If apprehended, he simply spread out his sketches for inspection and was set free. No one looked closely enough at the sketches to detect the position of army units on the drawing of a mountain range, or the outline of a fortress and gun emplacements on the design of a butterfly wing.

BADEN-POWELL AS A SPY

Sketch of a butterfly? No! A camouflaged drawing of a fort.

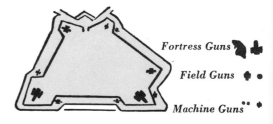

Fortress Guns

Field Guns

Machine Guns

AFRICAN ADVENTURES

Old Scout

BP

Wolf Cub

Boy Scout

*Early uniform
designs by Baden-Powell*

In 1895, Baden-Powell returned to Africa—this time to the Gold Coast where the Ashanti king, Prempeh, was defying the British authorities. In spite of orders against slave trading, Prempeh had been raiding neighboring tribes and had taken captives—not to be sold as work slaves, but to be used as human sacrifices. Baden-Powell was placed in command of a pioneering detachment to clear a road through the jungle to the Ashanti capital, in advance of the main army. When B.-P. approached Prempeh's "palace," the king meekly gave himself up to the British forces.

The trouble had hardly been settled in West Africa before new trouble arose in Matabeleland in southern Africa, in what is now Rhodesia. This was an entirely different kind of Africa. While the Ashanti campaign had been fought through swamps and deep jungle, the Matabele fighting took place in wild mountain country with countless hidden caves among towering boulders. Baden-Powell was so successful in tracking down and out-manuevering his enemies that the natives came to believe that he possessed super-natural powers. They gave him the name of "Impeesa"—"the-wolf-that-never-sleeps." It took almost half a year of campaigning to drive the Matabeles out of their mountain strongholds and force them to surrender.

Baden-Powell did not know it at the time, but his many varied activities had been preparing him for the event that would bring him world fame and recognition.

Differences in South Africa between the British government and the Boers of the Transvaal and Orange Free State had reached the breaking point. War seemed inevitable. Colonel Baden-Powell was ordered to raise two battalions of Mounted Rifles and proceed to the town of Mafeking, an important railroad center close to the Transvaal border.

The Boers declared war on October 11, 1899, and immediately laid siege to Mafeking. They met an unexpected, stubborn defense. For 217 days, Baden-Powell and his garrison of less than a thousand soldiers held out against an enemy force ten times as large. Every able-bodied man in town was made part of the defending force. Even the boys signed up and were put into a special cadet corps as bicycle messengers.

B.-P. afterwards called the siege of Mafeking "a game of bluff from start to finish." He used his vivid imagination to devise means for making the Boers believe that his fortifications were much stronger than they were. When he ran out of dynamite for mining the approaches to the town, he continued "mining" them with boxes filled with sand. When he had no more barbed wire for surrounding the town, he continued putting up posts and stringing non-existent "wire" that completely fooled the Boers.

From time to time, Baden-Powell struck out against the Boer line. The enemy never knew what to expect next and had to be on the alert continuously.

In this way, Baden-Powell kept a large force of Boers immobilized around Mafeking—a force that could have inflicted grave damage to the British Army units fighting the Boers elsewhere in several other scattered South African battle areas.

The courage and cheerfulness of their commander kept up the spirit of the people in the besieged town in spite of almost daily shellings that caused a great number of casualties. They even joked when the food supplies began to fail and horses' oats had to be used for bread and the horses themselves for soup meat.

For seven long months, all of Great Britain waited anxiously for news of Mafeking.

Finally, on May 17, 1900, Mafeking was relieved.

When the news reached the British capital the following day, the whole country went wild with joy. The name of Baden-Powell was on the lips of everyone. Queen Victoria made the defender of Mafeking, at 43, the youngest Major-General in the British Army.

From the defense of Mafeking

"THE HERO OF MAFEKING"

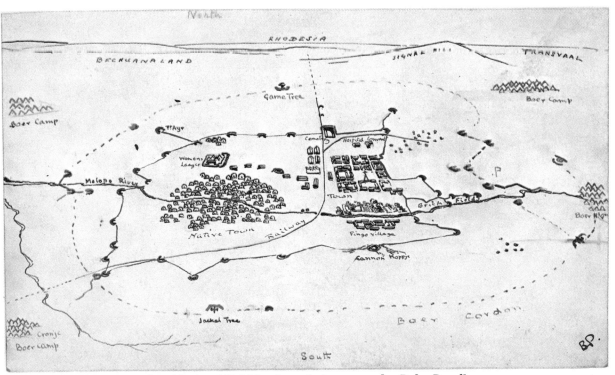

Map of besieged Mafeking drawn by its commander, Baden-Powell

THE START
OF THE
BOY SCOUT
MOVEMENT

When B.-P. returned to England in 1901 he was greeted everywhere as a hero. He soon learned that a small book he had written for army use, *Aids to Scouting*, was being read and avidly followed by the youngsters of Britain.

In 1903, he was invited by Sir William Smith, founder of the Boys' Brigade, to review a rally. It was attended by seven thousand boys out of a membership of fifty thousand.

Baden-Powell congratulated Sir William on the magnificent showing—but commented that he ought to have ten times as many boys, and would have them if there was more variety and attraction to the program.

"I agree with you," said Sir William. "Why don't you give us such a program? Why don't you rewrite your *Aids to Scouting* into a book for boys?"

B.-P. saw a real challenge in this. He set out to develop a program and to write and illustrate a handbook of activities. He searched for ideas on the training of boys through the ages, on physical fitness, on outdoor skills. But first and foremost, he drew on his own boyhood experiences and his adventures in India and Africa.

The world's first Boy Scout camp on Brownsea Island

Before making his "Boy Scout Scheme" public, he decided to try it out. In August, 1907, he took twenty boys to Brownsea Island in Poole Harbor, off the southern coast of England, for the first Boy Scout camp the world had ever seen. The scheme worked!

In January, 1908, his book, *Scouting for Boys*, began to appear in the bookstores and on the newsstands in England in pamphlet form, one part every two weeks. It was published in book form on May 1, 1908, and became an instant best seller. Boy Scout patrols sprang up all over England and, before long, were being formed in other countries.

It became evident to Baden-Powell that he had created

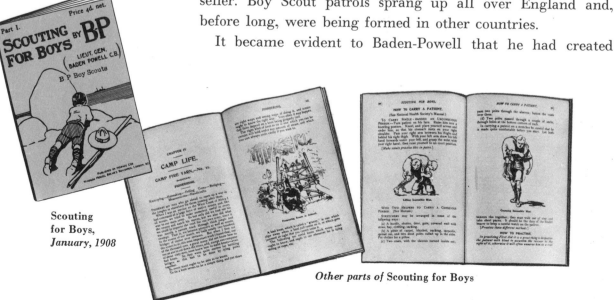

Scouting
for Boys,
January, 1908

Other parts of Scouting for Boys

something important that would require his complete attention. In 1910, he retired from the British Army to devote himself entirely to the movement he had founded—a movement that rapidly circled the globe.

To strengthen the world-brotherhood idea, Baden-Powell traveled extensively around the world and in 1920 called Scouts from all nations where the movement had taken root to a World Jamboree in London. It was during this first world gathering of Scouts that B.-P. was acclaimed "Chief Scout of the World." And it was in this capacity that he was greeted enthusiastically at other World Jamborees—in 1924 in Denmark, 1929 in England, 1933 in Hungary, 1937 in Holland— and was honored by many countries. The significance of his work was recognized to the fullest by his own country in 1929 when he was made a baron and became Lord Baden-Powell of Gilwell.

At the age of 80, Baden-Powell retired to Africa to spend his remaining days in the country he loved so well. With his wife, Lady Baden-Powell, World Chief Guide, he settled in Nairobi, Kenya. Here he died on January 8, 1941—a month and a half before his eighty-fourth birthday.

CHIEF SCOUT OF THE WORLD

Early Days in America

SCOUTING REACHES THE UNITED STATES

WILLIAM D. BOYCE was not the only American who had become convinced of the importance of Scouting to the youth of America. Copies of Baden-Powell's book, *Scouting for Boys*, had reached the United States even before the incorporation of the Boy Scouts of America, and men interested in boys had made the first attempts to help establish Boy Scout troops.

Prominent among these men was Edgar M. Robinson of the National Organization of the Young Men's Christian Association.

In his capacity as Secretary of the Committee on Boys' Work, Robinson had had occasion to follow the growing interest in Scouting among boys in many parts of the country and had had to cope with numerous letters asking about this new "Boy Scout thing." While the Y.M.C.A. was not in a position to take on Scouting on a national basis, it was able to help boys locally get the benefit of the Scout program. Robinson had already, in 1909, informed local Y.M.C.A.'s how they might be of assistance. Considering what had been happening since then, Robinson realized that some drastic steps had to be taken.

Robinson had become concerned at seeing several Scout associations springing up that competed with each other: "Boy

Scouts of United States," "National Scouts of America," "Peace Scouts of California," and various others—and, in formation by a chain of newspapers, the "American Boy Scout." Some of these groups were of a military or otherwise undesirable character.

Robinson was convinced that if the purpose of the Boy Scout movement was to be realized in America, there should be one single, strong, national organization, completely dedicated to the original ideals and program of Scouting as formulated by Baden-Powell. When Robinson learned that a group named "Boy Scouts of America" had been incorporated, he decided that this legally established corporation might be the nucleus of the single organization he envisioned.

With a couple of Y.M.C.A. colleagues, Robinson went to Chicago to see Boyce in the hope of persuading the publisher to his vision, and to offer the co-operation of the Y.M.C.A. in getting the organization under way.

EDGAR M. ROBINSON

Boyce quickly saw the importance and wisdom of Robinson's suggestions. He consented to go along and even agreed to pay a thousand dollars a month for the first months to finance the establishment of Scouting as a national movement.

Robinson hastened back to New York, met with some friends interested in boys' work, lined up with them a list of men who should be invited to help make one national Boy Scout organization a reality, and sent out invitations to a meeting.

On June 21, 1910, in the Board Room of the International Committee of the Y.M.C.A. at 124 East 28th Street, New York, a group of men of national reputation and with experience and interest in work for boys gathered to determine what steps might be taken to create the movement that Robinson so earnestly advocated.

Here were men representing thirty-seven different organizations concerned with boys—Y.M.C.A., Y.M.H.A., Playground Associations, Big Brother Movement, Public School Athletic League, existing Boy Scout groups, boy organizations such as the "Woodcraft Indians," the "Sons of Daniel Boone," and several others—as well as businessmen, educators, authors, editors and publishers.

Out of this meeting came the decision to proceed with the creation of a permanent organization, national in scope, and a committee to nominate the men who should head it. This Committee on Organization, with Ernest Thompson Seton of the "Woodcraft Indians" as chairman, immediately went to work. To handle the ever-increasing volume of requests for

Sketches by Ernest Thompson Seton

information and help, John L. Alexander of the Philadelphia Y.M.C.A. was made Managing Secretary.

The Committee on Organization succeeded in bringing into the new movement other existing boys' groups and the other Boy Scout organizations (with the sole exception of "American Boy Scout"—later dissolved following court action). It also formulated a set of bylaws, and persuaded a large number of men of national prominence to associate themselves with the movement as members of a National Council—with the president of the United States, William Howard Taft, as Honorary President, and Theodore Roosevelt as Honorary Vice President and Chief Scout Citizen.

On October 25, 1910, the original incorporators met and elected a Board of Managers, and on October 27, 1910, the Committee on Organization, its work done, handed over to this board its records and holdings. Colin H. Livingstone was elected President and Ernest Thompson Seton, Chief Scout. Daniel Carter Beard of the "Sons of Daniel Boone," Adjutant-General William Verbeck, formerly of the "National Scouts of America," and Colonel Peter S. Bomus, of the "Boy Scouts of the United States," became the first three National Scout Commissioners.

The Boy Scouts of America was, at last, firmly established as a functioning, independent organization, dedicated to the welfare of the American boy—and with an enormous amount of work ahead of it if it were to live up to its promise.

To direct this work, the Board of Managers—renamed Executive Board—chose a young Washington attorney by the name of James Edward West.

Three men were to have a tremendous influence on the early development of the new movement: Seton and Beard—both, like Baden-Powell, outdoorsmen, artists, and authors—and West, the administrator.

ERNEST THOMPSON SETON

ERNEST THOMPSON SETON—a tall man with a shock of unruly hair and a bushy mustache—was born in England in 1860 but emigrated to Canada at an early age. The wilderness of the American continent excited him to such an extent that he decided to become a naturalist. While working in this capacity for the provincial government in Manitoba he picked up another interest: a desire to help perpetuate the lore of the American Indian.

Coming to the United States, Seton combined his knowledge of nature with his writing and illustrating abilities to create a number of highly successful books—*Wild Animals I Have*

Known, The Biography of a Grizzly, Lives of the Hunted, Two Little Savages, and others.

His Indian interests led him to establish a youth organization which he called the "Woodcraft Indians"—with a code based on Indian tribal laws and a program of Indian games, skills and rituals. The purpose of the organization was "to give the young people something to do, something to think about, and something to enjoy in the woods, with a view always to character building—for manhood, not scholarship, is the first aim of education."

His rich background of woodcraft, camping, and other outdoor skills made Seton a logical choice for a Chief Scout of the new organization—the Boy Scouts of America. He remained Chief Scout for five years, adding immeasurably to the excitement and picturesqueness of the Boy Scout program.

DANIEL CARTER BEARD—later affectionately known by all Boy Scouts as "Uncle Dan"—was a man of medium height, with a clipped mustache and neatly trimmed goatee. He was born in Ohio, in 1850, but soon after moved to Kentucky—a territory rich with the legends of Daniel Boone.

UNCLE DAN

Dan had his mind set on an art career, and after the Civil War he arrived in New York to study at the Art Students' League. His magazine and book illustrations became so popular that he was chosen to illustrate Mark Twain's *A Connecticut Yankee in King Arthur's Court*.

Beard had brought with him to New York the recollections of a lively boyhood spent in woods and fields, and a love for the skills and the spirit of the pioneers who had opened up the western frontiers. He shared this heritage with all American boys through articles and drawings in the pages of *St. Nicholas Magazine* and *Youth's Companion*. These articles were later published in book form in the popular *American Boys' Handy Book* and *Outdoor Handy Book*. Beard also wrote and illustrated the *Buckskin Book for Buckskin Men and Boys*.

As a further step to keep alive the traditions and activities of the "American Knights in Buckskin" and "to educate our lads early in life to an appreciation of the absolute necessity and value of our forests and natural resources" he formed "The Society of the Sons of Daniel Boone."

When the Boy Scouts of America came into being, Dan Beard joined it enthusiastically as National Commissioner and Chairman of the National Court of Honor, and wrote and illustrated articles for the Boy Scout magazine, BOYS' LIFE, until his death in 1941, ten days before his 91st birthday.

Drawings by Dan Beard

THE STORY OF
JAMES E. WEST

WASHINGTON
CITY ORPHAN ASYLUM

THE STORY OF JAMES E. WEST is the American dream come true—the story of a crippled orphan who became the inspiring leader of millions of active American boys.

Jimmy was born in 1876—in the hundredth year of America's independence—in Washington, D.C. His early years were full of tragedy. His father died before Jimmy was born. When he was six, his mother was forced to put him in an orphan home while she went to the hospital. Within a year she was dead of tuberculosis, leaving Jimmy without any known relatives.

In those days, Jimmy was healthy and straight. But shortly afterward he began to limp and complained of pains in one hip. The people in charge of the orphanage thought the boy was faking to get out of work. He was whipped—but his leg got no better.

At last he was sent to a hospital where the doctors diagnosed a tubercular hip. Jimmy was kept in the hospital for nearly two years—much of the time strapped to a board with weights on his leg. He was finally pronounced an incurable cripple and sent back to the orphanage. He was now so lame that he could not do the work the boys were supposed to do—and so was given the bitter task of sewing and mending with the orphan girls.

When he was twelve, an old friend of his mother came to see him. She was Mrs. Ellis Spear, wife of the United States Patent Commissioner, and a writer of children's books. She gave Jimmy one of her books and invited him to visit her home. For the first time in his life Jimmy was taken into a family circle with five vigorous children. Mrs. Spear aroused his interest in reading and spurred his determination to secure an education. At the age of sixteen, Jimmy asked the matron of the orphanage for permission to go to high school—something unheard of for orphan children in the 1890's. After some persuasion he was given his wish—provided he did not let his work in the orphanage suffer. It meant working afternoons and evenings and getting up at 2 a.m. one day a week to do the laundry.

Jimmy was well liked by his school friends. He became editor of the school paper and, in spite of his crutches, business manager of the school's football team.

By the time Jimmy graduated from high school, the orphanage was paying him a small weekly fee in addition to his lodging and board. But he needed to earn more money if he were to get the education he desired.

One day he applied for a job at a bicycle shop.

The owner looked at Jimmy's crutches.

"I do need a bookkeeper," he said, "but I must have someone who can ride a bicycle."

"If I learn, may I have the job?" the boy asked.

The proprietor looked at the determined youngster.

"If you learn," he said, "you can have the job."

Within forty-eight hours the boy was back. His body was black and blue, his crippled leg cut and scratched from his falls off a borrowed bicycle. But he could ride—and the job was his.

By now Jimmy West had made up his mind to become a lawyer. He got the chance to go to law school and to read law with an attorney. To support himself he secured work at the Washington Y.M.C.A. and as a government stenographer.

After graduating from law school at 25, young West was appointed to the Board of Pension Appeals and later was made an assistant attorney in the Department of the Interior. At last he could afford good clothes and decent quarters—and even a secondhand automobile.

That automobile came to play an important part in his life.

One day, coming out of his office, West found his car gone. A policeman approached him.

JIMMY'S FIRST JOB

"We have your car," he said, "it is down the street. I just stopped a boy from stealing it. The case will come up in court tomorrow."

West was in court the next day when the boy was brought in—a scared youth in his early teens. When the young lawyer learned that the boy was without counsel he asked permission of the court to represent the boy.

"This is highly irregular," said the judge. "But . . . permission granted."

A few moments later, West had proved to the court that here was no question of theft but only of a boyish prank—he had himself been carrying the car ignition key in his pocket when the "crime" was being committed. The boy had merely sat at the wheel steering while the other members of his gang had pushed the car.

Case dismissed.

West was shaken by the thought that under existing laws a boy might have been sent to jail for childish mischief. He set out to get Congress to establish a Children's Court for the District of Columbia and threw himself into other work for youth.

This work made him aware of further needs of children—not only in Washington but in the whole country.

Boldly, he approached the President of the United States, Theodore Roosevelt, and persuaded him to call a conference on child care. West served as secretary of the conference, conducted all the preliminary work in connection with it, and was mainly responsible for its success. "But for you there would have been no conference," Theodore Roosevelt wrote to the young lawyer. "I have always thought well of you, but now I feel that you are one of those disinterested and patriotic citizens to whom this country stands under a peculiar debt of gratitude." Out of this first White House Conference on the Care of Dependent Children, organized by West, eventually came the Children's Bureau of the Department of Labor.

It was this experienced youth worker, now thirty-four years old, who was asked by the Executive Board of the newly formed Boy Scouts of America to head the movement.

West was preparing to enter a large Washington law firm at the time. His first thought was to turn down the Boy Scout offer. His second thought was: "I will give it six months—that should be enough to get the movement firmly established."

On January 2, 1911, West opened a national Scout office in the Fifth Avenue Building, 200 Fifth Avenue, New York, and went to work.

THE FIRST CHIEF SCOUT EXECUTIVE

*James E. West taking the salute
at a world jamboree*

But the six months he had planned to give to Scouting extended into thirty-two years of devoted and dynamic service to the boyhood of America as Chief Scout Executive and to the boyhood of the world as one of the most highly esteemed leaders in world Scouting.

Through all these years, West was never completely well. His tubercular hip often caused him excruciating pain. In spite of his handicap, he gave his energy, his vision, and his life to guide the destiny of the Boy Scouts of America. He built it from a struggling organization, competing with many other youth organizations, into a firmly established part of the American scene and watched it grow from a membership of 30,000 in 1911 to more than 1,500,000 in 1943 when he relinquished his active leadership. As Chief Scout, he continued his work in Scouting until his death in 1948.

West's accomplishments as Chief Scout Executive is an outstanding proof of the truth of Ralph Waldo Emerson's contention, "An institution is the lengthened shadow of one man." The Boy Scouts of America is indeed the "lengthened shadow" of one man—James E. West.

ELBERT K. FRETWELL

ARTHUR A. SCHUCK

Upon West's retirement as Chief Scout Executive, the Executive Board of the Boy Scouts of America chose a prominent educator to become his successor—Dr. Elbert K. Fretwell of Teachers College, Columbia University.

Fretwell prided himself on having been born "a Missouri dirt farmer"—but he left the farm in his youth and set out to see the world. His excellent voice and his extraordinary memory made him turn to the stage—not only in Shakespearian parts but as a singer in Wagnerian opera.

The stage palled—and Fretwell took up teaching. Here he found himself in his true element. After a few years as high school principal he joined the faculty of Columbia University as a professor of education and became widely known in educational circles. His interest in camping and outdoor living caused him to organize the first training course for camp leaders in the United States and to direct it for eighteen years at Teachers College.

His association with Scouting had begun early. For many years Fretwell had been active in the training of Scout leaders and as a member of the national Executive Board. As Chief Scout Executive for five years, he brought to the Boy Scout movement his intense interest in training—helping boys become better Scouts, and men better leaders.

Fretwell was followed in the top position of the Boy Scouts of America by a man who had grown up in Scouting—Arthur A. Schuck.

Schuck joined the Scouts in his late teens and soon after, in 1913, found himself the Scoutmaster of an extremely active troop in Newark, New Jersey.

Everything connected with Scouting excited him—the life in the open, the character values of the training, the citizenship aspects of the program. When, a few years later, he had a chance to make Scouting his lifework as a professional leader, there was no doubt in his mind about what course to take. He became Scout executive in Lancaster, Pennsylvania, at the early age of 22.

His outstanding executive ability soon came to the attention of James E. West, the Chief Scout Executive. West showed his faith in Schuck by making him, at 24, regional executive of the area comprising Pennsylvania, Delaware, Maryland, Virginia, and the District of Columbia. Three years later, West brought Schuck into the National Office as a member of the Field Department specializing in finance and organization.

When in 1931 an Operations Division was formed to deal

with the ever-increasing number of local councils, Schuck was chosen to head this important division. He performed his task with great effectiveness until 1944 when he was selected by the Los Angeles area as Scout Executive to handle the intricate details of reorganizing this important council.

It was from this job that Schuck was called to the National Council in 1948 to become Chief Scout Executive—a position he has filled with outstanding vigor and skill.

Under his leadership the Boy Scouts of America set out on a crusade to "Strengthen the Arm of Liberty"—to bring to the American people a greater awareness of the importance of the Scout movement to the American way of life and to provide more and better Scouting to an increasing number of boys.

This and subsequent crusades as well as other spectacular program features—national Good Turns, national jamborees, and participation in world jamborees—have had a profound effect on the Boy Scouts of America and have helped to raise its membership to the five-million mark.

Schuck's leadership has also extended into world Scouting. During his administration, several overseas Scout organizations have been assisted through the World Friendship Fund of the Boy Scouts of America and many foreign Scout leaders have been trained in American methods at American Boy Scout training centers.

Ceremony below the Statue of Liberty to open "Strengthen the Arm of Liberty" crusade

Shaping the American Program

THERE WAS EVERY REASON why Baden-Powell's "Boy Scout Scheme," as expounded in his book, *Scouting for Boys*, should have become an immediate success in England. It was created by one of the most famous Britishers of his day—the "Hero of Mafeking," idolized by all his countrymen. It featured everything that was exciting to a British boy—adventures in the farthest outposts of the empire, in India and Africa. It challenged every boy to follow in the footsteps of famous British heroes—Nelson and Drake, Cook and Clive, Livingstone and Ross. It held high the chivalry of King Arthur and Richard the Lion-Hearted.

THE APPEAL OF ADVENTURE

But why should Scouting catch on as it did, far beyond the borders of Great Britain, and set out on the triumphant conquest of the whole world?

Because it had in it the universal appeal to boyhood of adventure, of action, and challenge. Scouting was presented as a game that any red-blooded boy would want to play for the sheer joy there was in it—a game based on the activities of manly men: explorers, backwoodsmen, hunters, frontiersmen, pioneers, and seamen—full of the excitement of tracking and stalking, axemanship, fire building, life in the open.

Because it contained a code that appealed to a boy's inborn sense of honor and duty—of self-discipline, chivalry, sacrifice, service—and provided an outlet for his inherent "gang" instinct by making him a member of a "patrol" and a "troop."

Because boys—perhaps without consciously realizing it—approved of its aims. Baden-Powell opened his book with these words: "I suppose every British boy wants to help his country in some way or other. There is a way by which he can do so easily, and that is by becoming a Scout." A simple appeal, readily understood by a boy. But behind it—and understood by every adult—the purpose of Scouting: to improve the standards of the growing generation in citizenship, in character, in health and strength, in the ability to use hands and mind, in service to others.

Character

The biggest task that lay before James E. West, on taking over the leadership of the Boy Scouts of America as Executive Secretary in January 1911, was to shape, out of the Boy Scout scheme created by Baden-Powell, an American movement with an American program acceptable to American boys.

He went about this in a way that was characteristic of all his work in the Boy Scouts of America: he called to his aid men outstanding in the fields that needed to be investigated and acted on.

Fitness

At the first annual meeting of the Boy Scouts of America in Washington, D.C., a month after West took office, he proposed the establishment of four committees for getting the job done. These committees were appointed on February 14, 1911. The areas in which they were to work were:

Standardization of the Scout Oath, Scout Law; Tenderfoot, Second Class, and First Class Requirements.
Badges, Awards, and Equipment.
Permanent Organization and Field Supervision.
Finance.

Skill

Of these committees, the Committee on Standardization had the greatest immediate responsibility and the greatest opportunity for influencing the future of Scouting in America. The members realized the importance of writing the Scout Oath and Law in such language that they could be readily grasped by boys and become a part of their daily thinking in work and play, and of making the Scout requirements so attractive to the American boy that he would eagerly want to meet them.

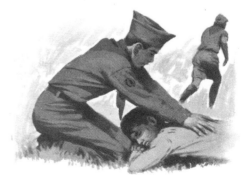

Service

BUILDING A
CODE FOR BOYS

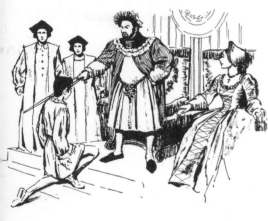

In Americanizing the Scout Oath and Law, the Committee was fortunate in securing for chairman Professor Jeremiah W. Jenks of New York University. Professor Jenks was fully aware of the Committee's great responsibility, and West, as secretary of the Committee, was determined to bring into the Oath and Law all the important human qualities that would be vital and meaningful to a boy.

In developing the code of his "scheme," Baden-Powell had studied the codes of man through the ages—the codes of the early Britons, Danes, and Anglo-Saxons; the oath of the Athenian youths; the law of the knights of the Middle Ages; the manhood codes of the American Indians, the African Zulu, and many others. From this study he had formulated the Scout's Oath and the Scout Law.

Baden-Powell's Scout Oath read:

> *On my honour I promise that I will do my best*
> > *To do my duty to God and the King;*
> > *To help other people at all times;*
> > *To obey the Scout Law.*

His Scout Law consisted of nine points:

1. A Scout's honour is to be trusted.

2. A Scout is loyal to the King, and to his officers, and to his parents, his country, and his employers.

3. A Scout's duty is to be useful and to help others.

4. A Scout is a friend to all and a brother to every other Scout.

5. A Scout is courteous.

6. A Scout is a friend to animals.

7. A Scout obeys orders of his parents, patrol leader, or Scoutmaster without question.

8. A Scout smiles and whistles under all circumstances.

9. A Scout is thrifty.

The Committee on Standardization held a great number of lively meetings during March and April 1911—once it was in session for ten successive days. Its work culminated in May, 1911, when, at West's insistence, the revised Scout Oath, Law and requirements were sent out to five hundred educators—university presidents and professors—with requests for criticisms and suggestions.

The Committee gave much consideration to a possible substitute for the term Scout "Oath"—investigating the exact meanings of such synonyms as "promise," "pledge," "vow," and several others.

I WILL DO MY BEST *by Norman Rockwell*

"It was agreed," the secretary finally reported, "that the word 'promise' was not strong enough to grasp the imagination of the boys; that the word 'pledge' had been given a distinct temperance content, and that the word 'vow' had too much of a religious significance. Therefore, the word 'oath' was kept after due deliberation, it being thoroughly understood that the Scout Oath was not in any way like the oath taken in a formal court of law, but that it was more on the order of the knightly oath of the Middle Ages, where the knight pledged his word of honor to reverence his king as his conscience, and his conscience as his king."

THE AMERICAN SCOUT OATH

Out of the work of this committee came the American Scout Oath which has stood unchanged for fifty years:

Boy Scout
1916

On my honor I will do my best
   To do my duty to God and my country and to obey
      the Scout Law;
   To help other people at all times;
   To keep myself physically strong, mentally awake,
      and morally straight.

Besides simplifying the wording of Baden-Powell's original Scout Law by expressing each point of the law in a single word—"Trustworthy," "Loyal," "Helpful," and so on—the most notable change was the increase of the Law's nine points to twelve, with the inclusion of "A Scout is brave," "A Scout is clean," and "A Scout is reverent." Of these additions, Baden-Powell himself, later in 1911, incorporated "A Scout is clean" into the British Scout Law. For the full text of the Scout Law, turn to page 72.

The twelfth point of the American Scout Law—"A Scout is reverent"—was included on the insistence of James E. West. In his opinion no boy could grow into a true man and a true American citizen without a deep religious conviction.

"Think of the early history of America," he said. "Describe America as it differs from other countries. Read the Declaration of Independence. Read the Constitution. Familiarize yourself with the leaders who have been vital factors in the life of America. And you will find that the basis for instructing the youth of America is first, reverence toward God; second, faithfulness in their own religious convictions; and, third, respect for the convictions of others in matters of custom and religion."

The wisdom of West's insistence became evident over the years, as one religious body after another enthusiastically endorsed the Boy Scouts of America and adopted the Scout program in its youth work, whereas Scouting in many other countries received little or no support from national church authorities.

In the Americanization of the Scout requirements, the Committee quickly discovered that very little needed to be done—Baden-Powell had built well.

In his tests for Tenderfoot—in itself an American term—Baden-Powell had included knowledge of the Scout Law, Scout signs and salute, of the composition of the Union Jack and the right way to fly it, of four knots. The main changes were the substitution of a knowledge of the flag of the United States for knowledge of the British flag, and an increase of the required knots to nine.

The original Second Class tests were kept intact: one month's service as a Tenderfoot, basic first aid, elementary signaling, tracking, Scout's pace, fire building, cooking, savings, compass points—but to these were added the use of knife and hatchet and a requirement calling for satisfactory evidence that the boy "has put into practice in his daily life the principles of the Scout Oath and Law."

The American First Class requirements also closely followed the original: swimming, savings, signaling, fourteen-mile hike, advanced first aid, cooking, mapping, axemanship, judging, enlisting a new boy. To these were added a requirement on American trees and wildlife and, as for Second Class, another asking for evidence that the boy had lived up to the ideals of Scouting.

AMERICAN SCOUT
REQUIREMENTS

AMERICANIZING
THE SCOUT BADGE

*Original
badge 1910*

*American design
adopted 1911*

THE SCOUT
UNIFORM

While the Committee on Standardization was working on the Scout Oath and Law, the Committee on Badges, Awards, and Equipment was busy on the designing of an American Scout badge and an American uniform, and on the development of requirements and designs for "badges of merit."

The original Scout badge, designed by Baden-Powell, was based on the arrowhead—or fleur-de-lis—that indicates the north direction on the mariner's compass. The idea in adopting this was to suggest to the boy that a Scout should be as dependable as a compass and should point the way as surely. Under the arrowhead was placed a scroll with its ends turned up ("like a Scout's mouth, because he does his duty with a smile and willingly") and carrying the Scout motto, "Be Prepared."

The Committee decided to retain the basic design but, at Dan Beard's suggestion, to Americanize it by superimposing on it an American eagle and a modified American shield. The rough sketch submitted by Beard was turned into a finished design by Clifford H. Berryman, cartoonist for a Washington newspaper. After approval by the committee, the design was submitted to the U.S. Patent Office where it was granted a design patent on July 4, 1911.

The Committee was less successful in redesigning the uniform. Baden-Powell's original called for a colorful uniform consisting of a broad-brimmed hat; a brightly colored neckerchief; blue, khaki, or gray shirt; blue or khaki shorts; brown leather belt; dark-colored or khaki stockings; brown or black shoes. The committee kept the hat only, coming up with a design based on the military uniform current at the time in

*Baden-Powell's
original design
for the Scout uniform
1908*

*First attempt at
an Americanized
uniform in 1911*

40

the U.S. Army, with a khaki uniform coat with a high collar and four large bellows pockets, khaki breeches, khaki web belt, khaki-colored, stiff canvas puttee leggings reaching to just below the knees, and brown shoes. Within a few years this uniform was found unsuitable, and the National Council reverted to the traditional Scout uniform, with the characteristic neckerchief, the comfortable shirt, shorts or breeches, and the broad-brimmed Scout hat.

The Committee readily accepted Baden-Powell's system of "Badges of Merit" as one of the notable and distinguishing features of Scouting—providing a method of advancement in which individual achievement on the part of the boy was encouraged and given recognition. Of this feature of Scouting, Dr. James E. Russell, Dean of Teachers College, Columbia University, was later to say: "I would consider myself a prince among school men, if I could devise a school program in which the curriculum should appeal so directly to a boy's interests and the courses of study apply so serviceably to adult needs. Every task in Scouting is a man's job cut down to a boy's size. The appeal to a boy's interests is not primarily because he is a boy, but particularly because he wants to be a man."

The original eight "Badges of Merit" described in *Scouting for Boys*—Ambulance, Stalker, Pioneer, Signaller, Seaman, Cycling, Marksman, Master-of-arms—had already been raised to fourteen in the earliest publications of the Boy Scouts of America with the addition of badges for Fireman, Clerk, Gardener, Horseman, Electrician, and Musician. At the same time, the idea had been introduced for giving special recognition to Scouts earning certain numbers of badges: "Shoulder lines are awarded to any Scout who gains any six badges of merit; the 'Silver Wolf' to any Scouts who gain all fourteen."

The merit badges were now increased by the Committee to fifty-seven, the requirements were spelled out and designs were developed for embroidered badges.

The idea of giving recognition for certain numbers of badges earned was further explored and resulted in the establishment of the Life Scout, Star Scout, and Eagle Scout ranks:

"The life scout badge will be given to all first-class scouts who have qualified for the following five merit badges: first aid, athletics, life-saving, personal health, and public health. The star scout badge will be given to the first-class scout who has qualified for ten merit badges. The ten include the list of badges under life scout. Any first-class scout qualifying for twenty-one merit badges will be entitled to wear the highest

Stalker

Signaller

Ambulance

Pioneer

Master-at-Arms

Marksman

Seaman

Cycling

The original eight "Badges of Merit" 1910

BADGES OF MERIT

Present Eagle Scout badge

The first Eagle Scout badge 1911

ORGANIZATION AND FINANCE

THE *HANDBOOK FOR BOYS*

Cover and title page—Official Handbook 1910

scout merit badge. This is an eagle's head in silver, and represents the all-round perfect scout." (The required number of merit badges for Star Scout and Life Scout ranks was later reversed.)

The other two committees appointed at the first annual meeting in Washington had not been idle. The Committee on Permanent Organization and Field Supervision had formulated plans which eventually culminated in the establishment of local Boy Scout councils throughout America and the introduction of professional leadership, and the Committee on Finance laid the foundation for a sound fiscal policy and a procedure for financing the rapidly growing movement.

Throughout the months in which the four committees were occupied in their various tasks, the work of producing an American Boy Scout manual had progressed. For the text, West, working with an Editorial Board, had turned to leading specialists in numerous fields—ranging from camping to bird study, from first aid to conservation, from mapping to signaling. A decided American atmosphere was given to the book by the inclusion of sections on Indian lore and pioneer skills. The citizenship chapter featured the lives and accomplishments of American heroes and statesmen. As soon as the new Scout Oath and Law, requirements, uniform and merit badge designs were approved, the book went to press. The first printing of this new *Handbook for Boys* appeared on August 31, 1911.

From that moment, there was nothing to stop the onward sweep of the Boy Scout movement in America. The membership figures entered upon their steady upward climb.

In the beginning, the membership consisted of Boy Scouts only—twelve years old and over—and their leaders. But soon the older boys staying on in Scouting demanded and were given their own kind of advanced program—Sea Scouting first, then, years later, Air Scouting and Exploring. Boys younger than twelve clamored for a chance to join. They got their wish with the inauguration of the program of Cubbing (later changed to Cub Scouting) for boys in the age bracket 9 to 12 (subsequently lowered to 8 to 11). In each instance, the needs and the desires of the boys were carefully studied and the program specifically developed to serve the age group for which it was intended.

Today, half a century after the transplanting of Scouting to American soil, Cub Scouts, Boy Scouts, and Explorers march forward together in the largest volunteer organization of youth the world has ever known—the Boy Scouts of America.

FORWARD AMERICA *by Norman Rockwell*

Cub Scouting

THE IMMENSELY POPULAR PROGRAM for the younger members
of the Boy Scouts of America—boys 8 to 11—is called CUB
SCOUTING.

Why Cub Scouting? "Thereby," as the saying goes, "hangs
a tale." And again it is necessary to turn to Baden-Powell to
gain a full understanding of the development of Cub Scouting,
its terminology and many of its games and ceremonies.

**YOUNGER BOYS
WANT TO BE SCOUTS**

Almost immediately after the start of the Scout movement,
boys who were not old enough for admission into the Boy
Scouts showed up at troop meetings and Scout rallies. They
could see no reason why they should not be permitted to join
in the fun their older brothers were having.

It was quickly realized that to lower the Boy Scout age and
permit the younger boys to join would inevitably mean the
loss of many of the boys for whom the program was designed.
But the eagerness which the younger boys exhibited made it
equally evident that something had to be done to serve them.

Nevertheless, Baden-Powell hesitated. He encouraged a few
qualified Scoutmasters to experiment with ways of working
with boys below Boy Scout age. From these experiments came
a knowledge of the kinds of activities that appealed to younger

boys. It became obvious that "Junior Scouting" wouldn't do; a different program was needed and a different name.

A first attempt at a plan for younger boys in Scouting was published in the Headquarters Gazette of the British Boy Scouts Association in January, 1914, and the announcement was made of a handbook "shortly to be published."

"The name 'Junior Scouts' will never do as a permanent one," Baden-Powell wrote at the time. "It does for preliminary use as explaining the movement—but we must invent a name that will appeal to the small boys."

All the while, Baden-Powell continued groping for the "gimmick" around which a program for younger boys could be built.

He found it in a book written in America and first published in chapter form in the American *Saint Nicholas Magazine* for American children—but penned by a man who was probably the most British of British authors: Rudyard Kipling.

AN IDEA FROM KIPLING

In retrospect it is hard to believe that one of the most famous of children's classics—*The Jungle Book*, dealing with the adventures of a boy among the animals of India—was written among the hills of Vermont. But such is the case.

Kipling, born in India and educated in England, married an American girl and came with her to the United States for their honeymoon. For four years, from 1892 to 1896, the couple lived on young Mrs. Kipling's family estate at Brattleboro, Vermont. Here Kipling wrote some of the books that established his world fame and eventually led to the Nobel Prize in literature—the two *Jungle Books* and *Captains Courageous*.

In the nine magic chapters of Kipling's first *Jungle Book*, Baden-Powell found not only an adventure tale to hold the interest of the younger boys, but also suggestions for activities and ideals for guiding young boys toward good citizenship through play and make-believe.

The Jungle Book tells the story of Mowgli, man-child lost in the jungle when his village is attacked by Shere Khan, the ruthless tiger. He is found by the kind Mother Wolf who persuades Akela, the old wolf and head of the pack, to permit her to rear Mowgli with her own cubs. Baloo, the wise and easygoing bear, befriends Mowgli and teaches him the law of the jungle, and Bagheera, the proud and powerful black panther, trains the boy in the skills of hunting and jungle survival. When Mowgli is kidnapped by the Bandar-Log—the lazy, chattering monkey people—Baloo and Bagheera, joined by Kaa the python and Hathi the elephant, come to his rescue. In the end Mowgli kills Shere Khan and becomes the acknowledged master of the jungle.

Kipling was an old friend of Baden-Powell's and had early shown his interest in Scouting by writing "The Scout's Patrol Song." He readily agreed to permit Baden-Powell to use his jungle tales and his jungle characters as the basis of a program for younger boys.

Baden-Powell's book setting forth his new scheme for a young branch of the Scout movement appeared in 1916 under the title *The Wolf Cub's Handbook*. The program was referred to as "The Wolf Cubs," and a boy who joined a pack became a Wolf Cub. The pack was in the charge of an adult Cubmaster known as Akela. The Wolf Cub pledged himself to the Wolf Cub Promise and followed the Law of the Pack and the Wolf Cub Motto, "Do Your Best." The young Cubs were encouraged to strive toward the jungle virtues of vigilance, endurance, strength, and co-operation, as exemplified by Akela, Baloo, and Bagheera, and to despise the baseness of the Bandar-Log, Shere Khan, and his followers. Games suggested by Mowgli's adventures became regular features of pack meetings. The Grand Howl with which the young wolves greeted the real Akela when he took his place on the council rock became a beloved Wolf Cub ceremony. Among themselves, Wolf Cubs greeted each other by holding up two fingers of the right hand to imitate the alert ears of a real wolf cub—a greeting which, in the Winston Churchill version, became his famous "V-for-Victory" salute.

Although launched in England during the First World War, Baden-Powell's new program for younger boys met with immediate success. Because of the lack of manpower, with all able-bodied men at the front, many young women volunteered their services as Cubmasters. They proved highly efficient—not only in Britain but in other countries where the Baden-Powell program was adopted. For the first time, women became members of the Boy Scout movement—with telling effects.

The Boy Scouts of America showed an early interest in Baden-Powell's Wolf Cub program, and in 1919 the organization studied it thoroughly and considered the feasibility of transplanting it to American soil. There was some fear that Boy Scouting might be unfavorably affected if younger boys were brought into the movement; also, the program, as used in Britain (and in 32 other countries) did not seem quite right.

During the next few years, Wolf Cub packs patterned on Baden-Powell's English program sprang up in a number of

First sketches by Baden-Powell of Wolf Cub badge and Wolf Cub sign

Mowgli before Akela

communities throughout the country. Some of these caused embarrassment to local Scouting, while others helped to focus attention on the need of a program for the boy too young to become a Boy Scout. The latter was the case, for instance, in Seattle, Washington, where the proximity to a growing Wolf Cub program on the other side of the border, in Canada, had created an early interest in this new development.

The demands for a younger boy program sponsored by the Boy Scouts of America grew. Parents and institutions wanted it. Scoutmasters recommended it to take care of boy "hangers-on" below Scout age. Educational leaders expressed the opinion that the Scout movement, by virtue of its years of experience and its country-wide organization, had a definite obligation to undertake the task of providing such a program. Finally, it was obvious that something had to be done when little fellows of six began to ask, "Can't I be half a Scout until I am twelve?"

After careful consideration of all the aspects, the Executive Board of the Boy Scouts of America established a committee to study the younger boy problem and retained Dr. H. W. Hurt, well-known educator, to investigate the matter. The Laura Spelman Rockefeller Memorial Foundation made available a substantial grant for an investigation of the nature, interests, and needs of younger boys, and for the development of a program that would appeal to them while serving the purposes of Scouting, of citizenship training, and of character development.

In the creation of a Cub program for the American boy the policy was established of following international usage whenever possible. Thus, the name "Cub" for the boy, and "Cubmaster" and "Akela" for the leader were kept. So were the sign and salute, and, with minor modifications, the badge and the uniform.

But the program and the organization of American Cubbing became materially different from its British counterpart.

In Britain, many phases of Cubbing followed the pattern set by Scouting, but in America every effort was made to avoid the overlapping of Cubbing and Scouting. Where the emphasis in Scouting was "outing," the emphasis in Cubbing became "home-and-neighborhood"—using the natural neighborhood play unit and operating toward the home instead of away from it. Overseas, much of Cubbing was done on hikes with the Cubmaster. In America, whatever outdooring there was to be in Cubbing was concentrated on backyard fun and occasional family picnics. The family itself became the main focus of Cubbing, and parents joined in the activities of their boys.

AN AMERICAN PROGRAM FOR YOUNGER BOYS

It became evident from the start that the jungle motif of India was too foreign to the American boy to form the basis of a program that would appeal to him. Mowgli was therefore turned from an East Indian boy into an American Indian boy, and Akela became the chief of his tribe. Later, even this Indian motif was modified, and Akela became simply the Cub Scout name for a good leader. "Some of the people you may call Akela," the *Wolf Cub Scout Book* states, "are your father or mother, your teacher, your den chief, your Den Mother or Cubmaster, or anybody who is a good leader."

CUB SCOUT ADVANCEMENT

Recognizing the young boy's love of badges to show off, an advancement plan was included in American Cubbing—but this was radically different from Baden-Powell's system. The British Wolf Cub had a chance to earn a First Star by passing tests quite similar to the Boy Scout's Tenderfoot requirements, a Second Star by fulfilling requirements patterned on those for Scout Second Class, and proficiency badges by passing tests along the line of those for Boy Scout merit badges. Instead of using this younger-boy version of Boy Scout advancement, an ingenious program was developed for American Cubbing in which the boy advances within his age span—having the opportunity to become a Wolf Cub during his first year, a Bear Cub during his second, a Lion Cub during his third—and culminating in the Webelos requirements in preparation for becoming a Boy Scout. The ambitious boy who quickly completes the "achievements" for his age is given the chance to earn further badges—arrowpoints—by passing tests in numerous "electives."

A major development in the American Cub Scout advancement plan was the idea of placing it squarely in the hands of the family in the home—away from any "examiner approved by the local association." Cub Scout advancement in the United States became a boy-and-father or boy-and-mother relationship. The boy was to pass his tests before one of his parents, and the parent's signature was to be sufficient for getting the boy credited with his achievement.

Another major innovation was the deliberate introduction of women leaders into Cubbing—in the beginning rather gingerly, but soon enthusiastically when the consequences of this step became evident in the added strength of the movement. But instead of following the overseas practice of using the woman leader in place of a male Cubmaster, in America the mother of a Cub was to take charge of the home-centered work unit of the pack—as Den Mother for a small group of

Cub Scouts in a "den." The den was further to be served by a den chief—a Boy Scout from a nearby troop who would help the Den Mother plan the program and lead the activities.

The American version of the Wolf Cubs emerged slowly under the guidance of the committee of the Executive Board and a picked advisory group of twenty-two outstanding specialists in the youth field. The proposals were further studied by a committee of 13,500 "corresponding censors and advisors"—educators, social workers, and Scouters from all over the United States. No other such complete pooling of judgment and experience had ever been made in the building of a youth program—but the results amply repaid the work involved.

On August 1, 1929, the first official Cub packs were organized to test the new program. Based on the experiences of these packs, the program was made generally available to all Scout councils in 1933.

The new program was received with enthusiasm by boys and their parents. Its popularity has increased year after year, and Cub Scouting—to which the original term "Cubbing" was changed in 1945—is now generally recognized as being of great value in the development and training of the younger boys.

Original Den Mother uniform

THE HOME

Cub Scouting is a home-centered program. The father and the mother help their boy with his Cub Scout advancement and take part with him in the activities of the pack.

THE CUB SCOUT PROMISE

I, ..., PROMISE
TO DO MY BEST
TO DO MY DUTY
TO GOD AND MY COUNTRY,
TO BE SQUARE, AND
TO OBEY THE LAW OF THE PACK

THE LAW OF THE PACK

THE CUB SCOUT
   FOLLOWS AKELA
THE CUB SCOUT
   HELPS THE PACK GO
THE PACK
   HELPS THE CUB SCOUT GROW
THE CUB SCOUT
   GIVES GOOD WILL

THE
CUB SCOUT SIGN

THE CUB SCOUT
HANDSHAKE

THE
CUB SCOUT MOTTO
DO YOUR BEST

THE CUB SCOUT
SALUTE

THE DEN

The den—a small, natural neighborhood group
—is the work unit in Cub Scouting. It is guided
by a Den Mother and a Boy Scout den chief.

THE PACK

The pack is made up of several dens. It is sponsored by an institution and led by a Cubmaster
and one or more assistant Cubmasters.

Look down the side street of almost any American town or village some day after school is out. It will probably be teeming with youngsters at play. The girls may be moving about alone or with a friend or two—but not the boys. They will be chasing around in small groups, stopping occasionally to put their heads together to scheme what to do next. And off they speed again for fun or mischief—until their spurt of interest has burned itself out and they set off on another tack.

Cub Scouting has wisely adopted this natural neighborhood play group in its organization. The neighborhood group becomes the Cub Scout den and is given purpose and direction. In the den, boys from 8 to 11 learn the give-and-take of co-operative living and pick up skills that help their physical and mental growth. They build up loyalties to each other and pride in their little unit.

Somehow such a natural play group always seems to have a tendency to "hang around" one home more often than around the homes of other boys in the group. Dick's mother apparently has a special way with her as far as the boys are concerned—and so, Dick's mother becomes the natural choice for Den Mother. Before this, she probably had her hands full with the gang whenever it came around. Now, as Den Mother, her hands will assuredly be equally full, but she has a program to work with that requires the co-operation of all the parents of the boys in the den, and she has an older boy, a Boy Scout serving as a den chief, to help her run the den activities.

Cub Scout dens generally meet during the afternoon once a week, most often in the Den Mother's home. The den meeting is a happy hour filled with fun and exciting things to do. It may open formally enough, with some simple ceremony. But soon the program turns into a round of games and tricks and stunts and handicrafts.

The games depend on the den's meeting place. Games indoors in house or apartment will be the quiet kind, while games in backyard or garden will be full of physical activity.

Tricks and stunts, ranging from simple magic to dramatizations of Mowgli's jungle adventures, are important parts of every den meeting. So are easy handicrafts: making things of paper or wood, fixing up the meeting place, making costumes and disguises.

Many of these activities are designed to take care of the moment only—but some are meant to carry over into the home, and others look forward to the monthly pack meeting when all the dens that make up the pack come together.

THE ADVENTURE TRAIL *by Norman Rockwell*

WHEN PARENTS APPROVE their boy's application to become a Cub Scout, they also sign themselves up in Cub Scouting.

"As Cub Scout parents, we understand the Cub Scout program recognizes the home as the greatest influence in a boy's life. For our son to gain the most from his Cub Scouting experience, we will take part in Cub Scouting activities with him:

a. By instructing and assisting our son in completing his Cub Scout achievements and electives; and by approving his work when he has done a job that measures up to his skill and ability;

b. By attending monthly pack meetings regularly, and by taking part in other den and pack activities;

c. By assisting and co-operating with den and pack leaders, and by serving as leaders if called upon."

LIFE IN THE PACK

Of all of these parent-and-son activities in Cub Scouting, the monthly pack meeting is of special significance. It sets the pattern for the work in pack, den and home. It gives the boys the feeling that something important is happening, of being part of a large, active concern. It gives the parents a chance to see their boys in action and to share in their advancement recognition, to get to know their neighbors better and to work with them for the good of all the boys in the pack.

At a typical pack meeting the boys and their parents are greeted on arrival by the Cubmaster and Den Mothers and other leaders of the pack. Old friends meet again, new parents and boys are introduced. But shortly the meeting breaks up into two sections—Cub Scouts in one room, parents in another.

The boys spend a busy half hour with their Den Mothers, den chiefs, and assistant Cubmasters in final rehearsal of the stunts or skits they have prepared to perform before their parents; there may be costumes to be put on, props to be assembled.

In the meantime, the parents meet with the Cubmaster and members of the pack committee. The Cubmaster discusses the progress of the dens, the achievements of the boys, the plans for the future. Members of the committee present problems that may be facing the pack and suggest ways of solving them.

Everything is ready now for the main part of the meeting.

The Cub Scouts enter in parade formation. They may line up for a short ceremony and for showing how many they are, but for a moment only. Immediately after, they swing into action, singing their songs, playing their games, performing their stunts, putting on their skits.

When the skits are over, the room is darkened while the candles are lit on the ceremonial advancement board with the painted replicas of the Cub Scout badges. One after the other, the boys come up with their parents and are presented with the badges they have earned since the last meeting—the badges that tell of their progress in Cub Scouting.

The picture of a father and a mother watching their son receive the badge they have helped him earn, from the hands of his Den Mother and his Cubmaster, explains better than a thousand words what Cub Scouting is: a home-centered program for young boys, guided by enthusiastic volunteer leadership.

The den gives the "Grand Howl"

How do cub scout leaders prevent den meetings and pack activities from becoming "just more of the same old stuff"?

By using the "monthly theme" idea.

It is not too difficult to make up weekly and monthly Cub Scout meeting programs by basing them on the wealth of suggestions contained in the boys' own handbooks and in the leaders' manuals. But how much easier the task becomes when it is a matter of building a program around a theme such as "We're Indians Now" or "Off to Treasure Island!" or "Let's Explore Outer Space." Immediately all sorts of activities suggest themselves.

In the well-run pack, the themes for the whole year are decided on at a planning meeting with all den and pack leaders taking part. But they are sprung on the Cub Scouts by the month, one at a time.

"How many of you wish you could go digging for gold on Treasure Island?" asks the Den Mother.

Unanimous chorus of "I do!" "So do I!" "Me, too!"

"Now, how many of you know where Treasure Island is?"

Silence. No one seems to know.

"Would you like to find out?"

"Sure!" "You bet!"

The Den Mother brings out Robert Louis Stevenson's book and begins to tell the story. The excitement mounts.

THE MONTHLY PACK THEME

"Now who wants to be Long John Silver? Who'll be Jim Hawkins? Who'll we get to play that wicked Billy Bones? Who'll be pirates? And sailors? How will you get to look like them?"

The air is full of suggestions. "We'll need ragged pants!" "And striped shirts!" "And eye patches!" "And a pirate flag with skull and crossbones!" "And swords!" "And a treasure chest!" "And a pirate ship!"

The boys themselves, in their eagerness, have lined up their own program for a month—of handicrafts and digging into books and special activities—and have created a program of action for their parents as well: mothers to help in the dressing-up department, fathers writing scripts and making the necessary props.

A tremendous turn-out is assured for the pack meeting at the end of the month when the result of each den's efforts is put on display before the combined pack and the parents of all the boys.

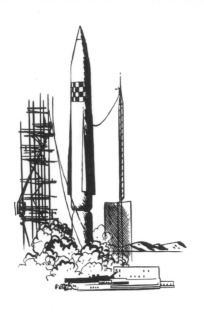

The enthusiasm will probably be equally high—especially among the boys—when, a couple of months later, the program is built around such an intriguing theme as "Space Travel."

To the surprise of fathers and mothers, the boys will most certainly wind up the month far better versed in the problems of space travel than they are. Every available picture on space ships will have been studied, every magazine story and newspaper article spelled through. Terms completely unknown in father's boyhood days will flow across the breakfast table; amazing calculations of take-off speed, thrust, and re-entry velocity will be bandied about; and distances to moon and sun and planets will be more readily quoted than the mileage to the next town.

UP INTO SPACE

But picking up new knowledge is just the starting point for getting into the pack theme of the month. Now this knowledge has to be put into tangible form. There are models and gadgets and charts to be made for the den's exhibit at the pack meeting, and there are props to be designed, and lines and action to be rehearsed for the den's part in the show that will be one of the main features of the meeting.

And again, as in all Cub Scout activities, fathers and mothers will be helping eager sons to master a new subject, to exercise their growing minds, to develop the ability of using their hands, to achieve a real sense of accomplishment.

ONE OF THE FUNCTIONS of den and pack meetings is to encourage each Cub Scout in his pursuit of "achievements."

The Cub Scout achievement requirements are planned with a definite purpose in mind. Some of them are designed to develop the boy physically, others to improve his mental powers. All of them take into consideration the boy's bursting physical energy—but also consider the limitations of the boy because of his age.

CUB SCOUT ACHIEVEMENTS

ACHIEVEMENTS

After having met the Bobcat requirements that make the boy eligible to become a Cub Scout he sets out to earn the badge in the rank to which

BOBCAT The Bobcat requirements are the simple tests that open the door of Cub Scouting to the eight-year old.

WOLF The Wolf badge may be earned by the eight-year-old Cub Scout. The den chief or the Den Mother

BEAR As soon as he is nine years old, the Cub Scout may go to work earning the Bear badge, whether he has

LION The Cub Scout of ten may work on Wolf and Bear requirements if he has not already earned the

his age entitles him. For each badge, the boy is required to perform twelve "achievements," each one planned with a definite purpose in mind.

Father and mother help their son read the explanations of the tests in his Cub Scout booklet—they,

too, find out what Cub Scouts do and, in this way, enter Cub Scouting with their boy.

may help the boy with his achievements, but it is his father or mother who watches him perform

them and who signs his Cub Scout book for the work he has successfully completed.

earned the Wolf badge or not. The difference between the requirements for Wolf and Bear is that

those for Bear are somewhat tougher to suit the boy's growing ability.

badges—or he may determine to set out directly for Lion rank. The requirements for the Lion badge

are an outgrowth of the Wolf and Bear requirements and follow the same pattern.

ARROW POINTS

FOR THE AMBITIOUS Cub Scout, there are more badges to earn beyond the Wolf Cub, Bear Cub, and Lion Cub badges by following the "electives" plan. This plan gives the boy a chance to advance further in Cub Scouting, to learn new things, and to win the coveted "Arrow Points"—the Gold Arrow Point for the first ten electives, the Silver Arrow Point for the next ten.

WOLF The electives available to a Wolf Cub range from making a secret code and drawing a simple picture to caring for a small garden, making a ship model, and doing a number of other things. The boy decides for himself whether he wants to do his electives in ten different fields or concentrate his efforts in a single field.

BEAR The electives for the Cub Scout of Bear Cub rank follow the same pattern as for Wolf Cub, but in each instance the subject matter is made slightly harder and a bit more specific. The electives are mostly home activities for which the Cub Scout needs the help of his father or mother and their signature upon completion.

LION When the Cub Scout of ten has earned his Lion Cub rank he, also, has arrow points to earn. Again, the requirements are slightly harder and further emphasis is placed on thinking of other people. When properly guided by his parents, the Cub Scout has the chance to explore many challenging and imaginative fields.

EVERY REGISTERED Cub Scout is entitled to wear the Cub Scout uniform of blue shirt, blue trousers or shorts, gold neckerchief, and blue cap with gold piping. In addition to its attractiveness and suitability for Cub Scout activities, there is symbolism to the uniform: blue for truth and loyalty and the sky above; gold for sunlight and cheer and happiness.

CUB SCOUT UNIFORM

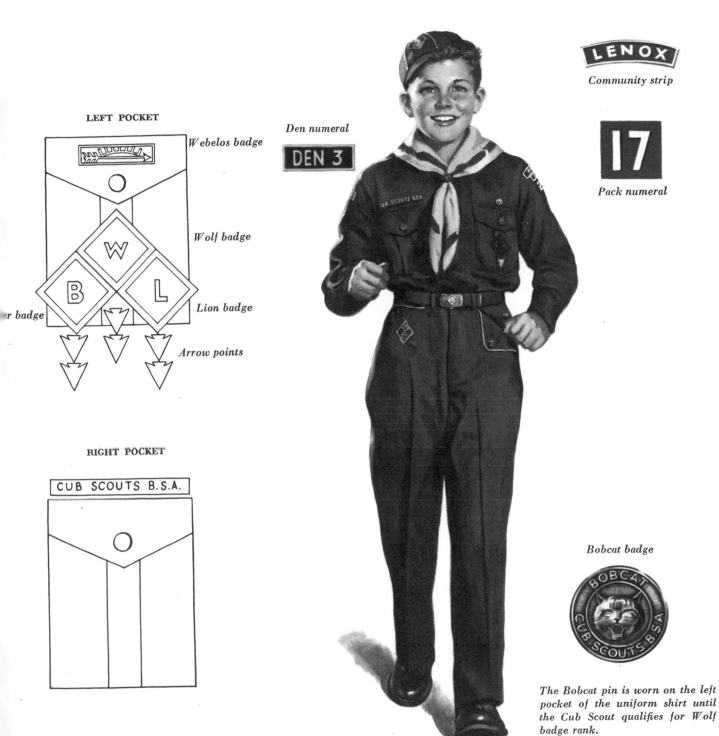

LEFT POCKET

Webelos badge

Wolf badge

Lion badge

Arrow points

RIGHT POCKET

CUB SCOUTS B.S.A.

Den numeral

DEN 3

LENOX

Community strip

17

Pack numeral

Bobcat badge

The Bobcat pin is worn on the left pocket of the uniform shirt until the Cub Scout qualifies for Wolf badge rank.

63

WEBELOS

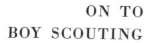

ON TO
BOY SCOUTING

WHEN THE CUB SCOUT nears his eleventh birthday he dreams of the big day when he can become a Boy Scout. While still a Cub Scout he has a chance to prepare himself for the occasion by meeting the Webelos requirements. The made-up word "WeBeLoS" suggests the boy's advancement: W for Wolf, B for Bear, L for Lion, S for Scout. It has, to the boy, a further meaning: "*We'll Be Lo*yal *S*couts."

To reach Webelos rank, the boy must be a Lion Cub Scout at least ten and one-half years old, know the Boy Scout Tenderfoot requirements, perform a service project for his home, his den or his pack, visit a troop, and get his Boy Scout membership application in readiness. In an active pack, all the boys who have reached the required age are gathered together in a special den—the Webelos Den. Here they are trained in all the skills that will make it possible for them to become Boy Scouts the day they reach eleven.

The recommended method is for the ground work of the transfer into Boy Scouting to be laid three months before the Cub Scout is eleven by the Cubmaster's informing the local troop that a boy will be ready to become a Boy Scout.

The boy's graduation is one of the most important ceremonies in Cub Scouting. It takes place in the pack meeting, with the boy's parents, his future patrol leader and Scoutmaster present. His investiture as a Tenderfoot Scout takes place at the first troop meeting following the boy's Cub Scout graduation.

MIGHTY PROUD *by Norman Rockwell*

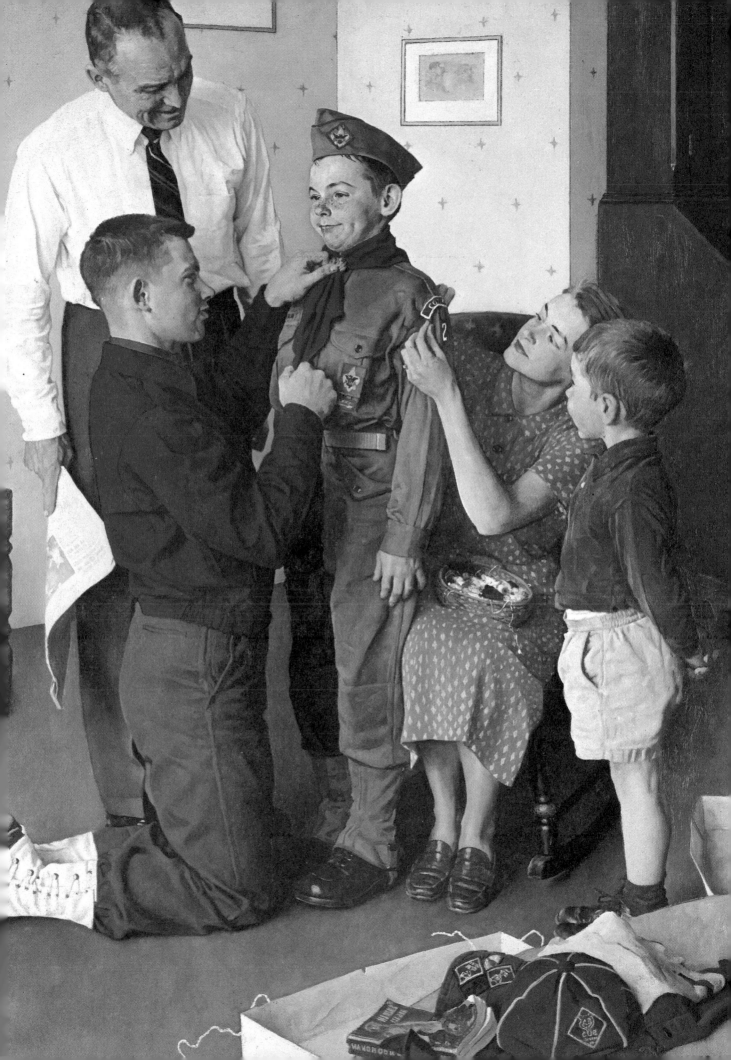

Boy Scouting

TODAY, half a century after the founding of the Boy Scout movement in the United States, it is a simple matter for an American boy of eleven or over to become a Boy Scout. If the boy has been a Cub Scout, he will probably join a Boy Scout troop related to the same institution that sponsors his Cub Scout pack. If he has not been a Cub Scout, he will have no difficulty finding a Boy Scout troop near his home—there are more than 60,000 of them, in practically every town and village in the country.

In the early days of Scouting, things were quite different. Scout troops and patrols were far apart. Many boys wanting to become Scouts had to follow the instructions in the first Scout handbook: "If there is no patrol near you, get some man interested enough to start one by giving him all the information."

Another problem that faced the boy who desired to join was the attitude of some adults not yet educated to the merits of Scouting.

Many people felt that Scouting was little more than a new-fangled "fad" that would fade away when the boys tired of it. Others had the unfounded notion that Scouting, calling for boys to put on a uniform, was "militaristic"—and in those days the tag of "militarism" was like a red flag to many who had followed the convulsions of Europe in numerous small wars and were wondering where the "powder keg" would blow up next. To still others, the Boy Scout slogan of "A Good Turn Daily" provided a never-ending source of helping-old-ladies-across-the-street jokes.

But the boys of those days—the pioneers of the Scout movement—went right on becoming Boy Scouts, shaking off the barbs of ridicule and misunderstandings. They went right on putting on the khaki uniform, hiking and camping and "helping other people at all times."

As the general public became better informed about Boy Scouting as valuable training for boys in physical fitness, character, and citizenship, the attitude began to change. And with the change in attitude came an awareness of the necessity of protecting the Boy Scout movement against encroachment and commercialization.

THE FEDERAL CHARTER

To provide such protection of the good name of Scouting and of the Boy Scout insignia and uniform, as well as to give public recognition to the movement, a bill was introduced in Congress in February, 1916, seeking a Federal Charter for the Boy Scouts of America. The bill passed both houses by unanimous consent and was signed into law by President Woodrow Wilson on June 15, 1916.

Within a year, the United States entered World War I. The importance of Scouting became even more evident. The Boy Scout uniform became the sign of a boy serving his country. More and still more boys joined the movement—in the short span of two years the Boy Scout membership doubled.

But it wasn't only the uniform that made the boys sign up. They joined for the same reasons that boys become Boy Scouts today. For the chance to play and work as team members in a Scout patrol and troop, for the opportunity to live an outdoor life, learning the Scoutcraft skills of hiking and camping, and for the purpose of meeting the manhood challenge of the Scout Oath and Law and the spirit of Scouting.

SCOUT TEAMWORK,
SCOUTCRAFT,
SCOUT SPIRIT—

then and now: the three-fold appeal of Scouting.

"THE PATROL SYSTEM," Baden-Powell said, "is the one essential feature in which Scout training differs from that of all other organizations, and where the system is properly applied, it is absolutely bound to bring success. It cannot help itself!"

Other youth organizations, before the start of the Boy Scout movement, had made use of outdoor activities and of some kind of code. But one feature gave Scouting its extra appeal. It was the method prescribed of forming six to eight boys into small fraternity-gangs—"patrols"—each under its own responsible boy leader, chosen by the boys themselves. Baden-Powell understood boys and wisely made use of their own natural way of organizing.

LIFE IN THE PATROL

The patrol idea has stood its test. It is the unit of Scouting, whether for work or play, for duty or discipline.

"The Scout patrol is the swellest boys' gang in all the world," says the Boy Scout *Handbook*. "A patrol is a team, with all the fellows playing the game of Scouting, with all of you working toward the same goal, all of you having a whale of a good time. And why shouldn't you? In the patrol you learn what it is to go hiking and camping with your best friends . . . to build your own fire and cook your own food . . . to swim, to dive, to paddle a canoe . . . to live your life according to the Scout code . . . to sit around a glowing campfire and sing and laugh together in real comradeship."

For a patrol to experience this kind of Scout life it needs to have a good patrol leader. Generally, the boys are able to judge for themselves which boy among them has the best qualifications and are smart enough to elect him their patrol leader. Chosen in this manner, the patrol leader has the confidence of

his boys and therefore the best possible chance for building up the patrol. He receives training for his job from his Scoutmaster and other troop leaders, and often through special patrol leader training conferences where experts on various phases of Scoutcraft demonstrate the skills of successful outdoor living.

Each Boy Scout patrol has its own identity—its own name, flag, emblem, and call, all of them with an outdoor atmosphere. Most patrols pick the name of an animal or a bird and become "Silent Panthers" or "Roaming Buffaloes," "Flying Eagles" or "Screaming Hawks." Whatever animal or bird the patrol fancies becomes its "totem" and provides the design on the boys' shoulder emblem and on the patrol flag, the mark on the patrol's equipment, and the secret call used to gather the patrol.

Patrols meet regularly in the homes of the boys, in the patrol's own den, or in the troop meeting room. Patrol meetings are busy occasions. There are new Scoutcraft skills to be learned, games to be played, songs to be sung. The patrol may have a handicraft project in the works—making patrol den furniture or camping equipment. And then there is planning for the future—for a stunt for the troop meeting, for a feast on the next hike, for the overnight camp at the end of the month.

The good patrol, under a well-trained leader, goes hiking and camping on its own from time to time. Those events are the high spots in the patrol's life. It is here that patrol spirit reaches its peak.

LIFE IN THE TROOP

THE PATROL is not a solitary boys' gang, going its own way. The patrol is a part of a Boy Scout troop—usually made up of from four to six patrols. The great advantage of this method of organization is that several patrols have a chance to match themselves against each other. In this way, all patrols are kept humming—each of them moved by the normal boy's desire to excel, to be the best in the troop in games and contests, in camping and advancement.

The program of the troop is planned in the patrol leaders' council. The Scoutmaster and other troop leaders determine the main lines, but it is up to the patrol leaders to bring to the council meeting the desires of their Scouts, and to agree on the details of the troop program. One of the important functions of the patrol leaders' council, as the *Handbook for Scoutmasters* points out, is "to give responsibility to the boy—since this is the very best of all means of developing character."

The quality of the troop program determines the effect that Scouting will have on each boy. It is only as the program meets the desires of the boy that it has a chance to hold him—and it is only by holding him that Scouting can influence the boy physically, mentally and morally.

Troop meetings are not "meetings" in the usual sense of

sitting down, listening to reports, following parliamentary procedure—they are periods of activity. There are fun games to shake the patrols together, skill games to test the patrols' Scouting abilities, Scoutcraft instructions followed by contests in the skills shown—and possibly a closing ceremony where recognition is given to Scouts who have reached a higher rank.

Troop hikes are also occasions for testing the skills of the patrols. The whole troop may have worked for a month on such an important subject as first aid; on the troop hike, each patrol is faced with a first aid "case" with moaning "victims" made up to look like the real thing. Or signaling may be the "big idea" of the month, calling for a climax event of sending a message by Morse from one hilltop to another.

Troop overnight camps similarly pit the patrols against each other in camping skills—tent pitching, fire building, cooking and all the other skills of good camping.

In addition to these regular events, the good Scout troop has numerous other events during the year—father-and-son hikes, parents' night, Boy Scout Week celebrations, Good Turns to the chartered institution or to the community. And, of course, the big event of the year: summer camp when all the patrols go camping together.

ON MY HONOR I WILL DO MY BEST
TO DO MY DUTY TO GOD AND MY COUNTRY
AND TO OBEY THE SCOUT LAW;
TO HELP OTHER PEOPLE AT ALL TIMES;
TO KEEP MYSELF PHYSICALLY STRONG, MEN-
TALLY AWAKE, AND MORALLY STRAIGHT.

THE SCOUT LAW

A SCOUT IS

TRUSTWORTHY. A Scout's honor is to be trusted. If he were to violate his honor by telling a lie, or by cheating, or by not doing exactly a given task, when trusted on his honor, he may be directed to hand over his Scout badge.

LOYAL. He is loyal to all to whom loyalty is due, his Scout leader, his home, and parents and country.

HELPFUL. He must be prepared at any time to save life, help injured persons, and share the home duties. He must do at least one Good Turn to somebody every day.

FRIENDLY. He is a friend to all and a brother to every other Scout.

COURTEOUS. He is polite to all, especially to women, children, old people and the weak and helpless. He must not take pay for being helpful or courteous.

KIND. He is a friend to animals. He will not kill nor hurt any living creature needlessly, but will strive to save and protect all harmless life.

THE SCOUT BADGE

OBEDIENT. He obeys his parents, Scoutmaster, patrol leader, and all other duly constituted authorities.

CHEERFUL. He smiles whenever he can. His obedience to orders is prompt and cheery. He never shirks nor grumbles at hardships.

THRIFTY. He does not wantonly destroy property. He works faithfully, wastes nothing, and makes the best use of his opportunities. He saves his money so that he may pay his own way, be generous to those in need, and helpful to worthy objects. He may work for pay, but must not receive tips for courtesies or Good Turns.

BRAVE. He has the courage to face danger in spite of fear, and to stand up for the right against the coaxings of friends or the jeers or threats of enemies, and defeat does not down him.

CLEAN. He keeps clean in body and thought, stands for clean speech, clean sport, clean habits, and travels with a clean crowd.

REVERENT. He is reverent toward God. He is faithful in his religious duties, and respects the convictions of others in matters of custom and religion.

THE SCOUT MOTTO
BE PREPARED

THE SCOUT SLOGAN
DO A GOOD TURN DAILY

THE SCOUT SIGN

THE SCOUT HANDSHAKE

THE SCOUT UNIFORM

The Boy Scout uniform is part of the romance of Scouting. It is a symbol of the ideals and outdoor activities of the movement.

The uniform, with badges to show his accomplishments, gives the boy pride in his appearance. Besides, the uniform makes him feel that he belongs, that he is truly a member of the world brotherhood of Scouting.

Community strip

OMAHA

Troop numeral

5

Patrol medallion

FROM THE MOMENT the new boy takes his first steps on the Scouting trail, he is introduced to the three features of all Scouting advancement: SCOUT TEAMWORK, SCOUTCRAFT, SCOUT SPIRIT.

The new boy receives his early Scout training in the patrol to which he expects to belong. Here he gets a taste of what it means to be a Boy Scout, how to play on the Scout team, doing his part to make the patrol a success. In patrol meetings and on patrol hikes he learns the first rudiments of Scoutcraft. He masters the Scout Oath and Scout Law and begins to pick up the spirit of Scouting.

TENDERFOOT

When the boy has met the simple Tenderfoot tests before his patrol leader and has been examined in them by his Scoutmaster, he is ready to be accepted into the Scouting brotherhood at a ceremony at a troop meeting or around a camp fire. The boy stands before his leader and his fellow Scouts, raises his hand in the Scout Sign and pledges himself to the Scout Oath. The moment the last words of the Oath have crossed his lips, he is one of the gang—a member of the largest movement for youth the world has ever known.

Simple Scoutcraft

The new boy dreams of going hiking and camping the moment he joins a patrol. To help him to become a good outdoorsman, his patrol pals set about teaching him the proper use of an axe, what precautions to take before building a fire, how to tie half a dozen important knots, how to reach the doctor, police, and fire department in case of an emergency, and how to care for a cut or a scratch.

The Flag of the United States

Every American should know the history of the flag of our country and how to display it. These are among the first things that an eleven-year-old must learn to become a Boy Scout. He is taught when to fly the flag, how to hoist it and lower it, how to fold it properly, how to salute it in uniform and as a civilian. In addition to these requirements, he must be able to recite the pledge of allegiance to the flag.

Traditions of the Patrol

To fit into his patrol and troop as quickly as possible, the new boy needs to know what makes them "tick." He is told the history and traditions of his patrol, and is taught how to give the patrol call. He meets his Scoutmaster and the other leaders of the troop and learns their duties and the part each plays in making the troop a success. He finds out what is expected of him as a member.

Uniform, Sign, and Salute

The new boy is eager to put on the Scout uniform he is entitled to wear as soon as he has passed his Tenderfoot tests. But first he must know about the importance of that uniform and about the badges he has a chance to earn and wear on it. He must also know how to wear the uniform properly and how to act in it—how to give the Scout sign, the Scout salute, and the left-hand Scout handshake.

Scout Oath and Law

The new boy learns the Scout Law as part of his Tenderfoot tests and explains each of its twelve parts to his Scoutmaster in his own words. "What does it mean that 'A Scout is trustworthy'?" "How can you prove that you are friendly?" When the boy has a clear understanding of the Scout Law, he is ready to take the Scout Oath—to promise on his honor that he will do his best . . .

Scout Motto and Slogan

Scout motto and Scout slogan go together—"Be Prepared" and "Do a Good Turn Daily." When a boy is prepared, he is better able to perform a Good Turn. "Prepared for what?" someone asked Baden-Powell. "Prepared for any old thing!" was the Chief Scout's reply—prepared for first aid, for saving the life of a drowning person, for fire, for flood, for lighting a fire in the rain, for "any old thing."

SECOND CLASS

No BOY SCOUT wants to remain on the lowest rung of Scouting—the Tenderfoot stage—for very long. As soon as he has joined his patrol he sets out to advance—first toward Second Class rank and, later, toward First Class and the higher Scout ranks: Star, Life, and Eagle.

In the good patrol and troop an active boy cannot help but advance. The various tests are so cleverly arranged that the normal activities of his gang carries the boy forward in the three advancement fields: SCOUT TEAMWORK, SCOUT-CRAFT, and SCOUT SPIRIT.

To show his Scout Teamwork as he works toward reaching Second Class rank, the Scout must prove himself a dependable member of the team by regular and whole-hearted attendance at patrol and troop activities—meetings, outdoor events, special projects. This is far more than just a matter of "being there." The Scout works with his friends in the patrol to make it the finest in the troop, he accepts whatever patrol duties come his way and carries them out to the best of his ability. He cooperates with the leaders of his troop to make his unit one of the very best in the district or the council.

The Scoutcraft skills for Second Class are all hiking skills which a boy picks up on the outdoor expeditions of his patrol and troop in the most natural way in the world: simply by doing them. While having the fun and excitement of hiking

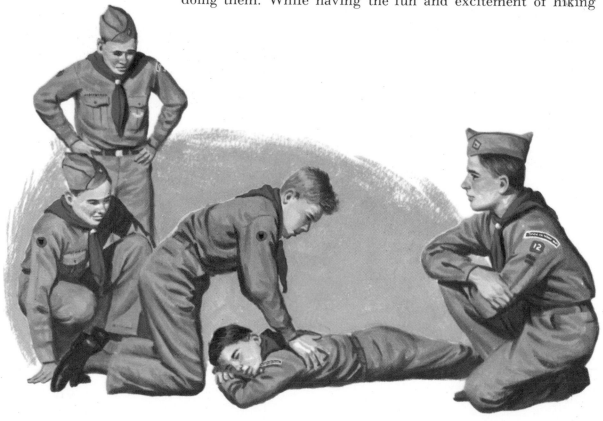

with his patrol under a trained patrol leader, the Scout has a chance to practice all the skills that are needed for a happy experience. He learns to pick the right kind of clothing and equipment, to find his way, to use his eyes and ears for observing wild animals and birds, to build a fire and cook a simple hike meal, to act correctly in an emergency.

When the Scout has become proficient in the individual Second Class Scoutcraft skills, he combines all of them into a single experience—the Second Class testing hike. He sets out with a companion or, possibly, with his whole patrol on a cross-country journey to demonstrate how thoroughly he is at home in woods and fields. The Second Class hike is an enjoyable occasion, a climax event growing out of the patrol activities that have gone before.

What goes for Scout Teamwork and Scoutcraft goes for Scout Spirit as well. Scout Spirit is the natural outcome of the boy's attempt to live up to the Scout Oath to which he pledged himself on joining, and the Scout Law he promised to keep. The expectations of his patrol pals and troop leaders challenge him to do his best as a Scout—but the attitude of his parents is equally important, and the help they are willing to give him. The more strongly a boy feels that he has the backing of his father and his mother in his Scout efforts, the harder he will work to prove himself a good Scout.

The boy passes his Second Class Scoutcraft tests before his patrol leader, usually on trips with his patrol or on special troop advancement hikes. When the Scoutmaster is satisfied that the boy has also met the tests in Scout Teamwork and Scout Spirit, he sends him before a troop board of review. This board consists of at least three members of the troop committee—men who are interested in boys and have a strong belief in Scouting as an important influence in the growth of boys. This board does not re-examine the boy but simply makes certain that all tests have been met according to the standards of the Boy Scouts of America.

The board certifies the Scout for advancement, and at an early troop ceremony the Scout is awarded a hard-earned Second Class badge.

"The longest journey," the Chinese say, "starts with but a single step." It is of the greatest importance for the Scout to reach Second Class rank as soon as possible after joining. When a boy has once tasted the thrill of Scout advancement he is well on his way toward higher and still higher ranks in Scouting.

Go Hiking

For a successful hike, there are things that a boy needs to know in advance, and preparations that must be made.

Hike clothing and equipment must be just right for the locality, season and weather, and for the kind of hike the patrol has planned. There is a right and a wrong way of walking for greatest efficiency—even a right and wrong way of resting along the way. There is safety to be practiced on highways and cross-country, and silent signals for use when moving noiselessly in a group. There are health measures to be taken to avoid poison ivy and other poisonous plants and to be certain that water is safe for drinking. And knowledge is required for reading a map, for following a compass, for measuring the distance covered.

Use Eyes and Ears

Some people go through life without noticing the wonders of nature around them—but not a Scout. The very word "to scout" means "to look for, to watch, to observe"—and in its original Latin form, *auscultare*, also "to listen to."

The ability to use eyes and ears is one of the most important phases of Scout training. For this nature provides the best training ground. A Second Class Scout is required to explore a stretch of nature—a field, a forest, a meadow or other natural area—study its wildlife and find out from his own observations how plant life and wild life live together. In addition, he must show his ability to read and follow the trail made by a fellow Scout or the tracks of an animal, or to stalk another Scout.

SECOND CLASS SCOUTCRAFT

Let's Eat!

A hike has a way of making a boy even more hungry than he gets at home. But on a hike he has no refrigerator to raid, no mother to do the cooking for him. He must do things himself. That means bringing the necessary foodstuffs from home and knowing how to prepare them in the open.

Several skills are involved in producing a hike meal: The Scout must know how to select the proper kind of tinder and kindling and fuel for his fire. He must be able to use knife and axe for preparing his fire wood. He must know how to clear the ground and to light a fire. He must be able to cook a quick hike meal. And, possibly, more important than anything else: He must know how to extinguish fire to the last spark.

Prepare for Emergency

"Safety through Skill" is an important Boy Scout emphasis. By doing what he has been taught, the Scout on a hike is rarely caught in an emergency involving himself. But he may find himself up against an accident involving somebody else—and is therefore expected to know how to handle the more common first aid cases. But also, whether on the hike or at home, he is supposed to be prepared for any eventuality.

He is required to show how to cope with "hurry cases" of arterial bleeding, stopped breathing, poisoning by mouth, and to demonstrate first aid for shock and fainting, cuts and scratches, burns and scalds, blister on heel, bites or stings of insects, skin poisoning from poisonous plants, sprained ankle, object in eye.

FIRST CLASS

BADEN-POWELL had this to say about the importance of becoming First Class: "A boy does not really get the full value of Scout training until he is a First Class Scout." And he gave the reason: "The tests for First Class Scouts were laid down with the idea that a boy who proved himself equipped to that extent might reasonably be considered grounded in the qualities which go to make a good, manly citizen."

The First Class tests follow the pattern of the tests for all Scout advancement—but for each step up in rank, the boy is expected to have grown, to be able to meet more demanding requirements.

In the Scout Teamwork tests it is no longer simply a matter of being present and taking part in patrol and troop activities, but also of showing leadership ability, willingness to take on special responsibilities. The Scout has a chance to be chosen patrol leader by his fellow Scouts, or to become troop scribe, librarian, or quartermaster if he has special abilities in these particular fields.

In Scoutcraft the boy moves from the skills of the hiker into the skills of the camper. He becomes a trained outdoorsman who knows how to put up camp and how to make himself comfortable in the open. He learns what equipment is needed for a successful experience, how to cook adequate meals over an open fire, how to keep healthy in camp. In addition, he picks up other outdoor skills—swimming for fun and fitness and safety, signaling for sending a message—and practices advanced first aid for taking care of emergencies.

As in the case of Second Class advancement, the Scout aiming for First Class rank winds up his Scoutcraft training with a climax event. This time it is a camping adventure— the First Class testing camp during which all the individual skills the boy has learned come into play.

But the most important part of First Class advancement is the Scout Spirit the boy has picked up since joining. By the time he reaches First Class, the Scout Law should have become part of his thinking and of the way he acts. The Scout motto— "Be Prepared"—should have become an incentive to him in learning still more Scoutcraft skills. The Scout slogan—"Do a Good Turn Daily"—should have become a spontaneous habit. His adherence to the Scout Oath should have made him realize more fully his duty to God, his country, and his fellow man, and should actually have helped him in his continuing efforts to become "physically strong, mentally awake, and morally straight."

Preparing for Camp

Part of the fun of camping is the anticipation of it, the preparing for it. Each Scout helps in the planning and is busy securing his personal camp equipment. In addition, each member works to get the patrol equipment in shape. A great number of ambitious Boy Scout patrols make their own tents and earn the money for buying the equipment they cannot make themselves. This involves a lot of work—but it also gives a satisfaction that can not be attained in any other way. And finally, when all the equipment is in shape, he learns to pack it properly.

**FIRST CLASS
SCOUTCRAFT**

Putting up Camp

The trained camper picks his camp site carefully and puts up his camp in the most proficient manner. The boy who camps regularly with his patrol and troop quickly learns to look at a stretch of ground and determine whether requirements of soil, slant, shelter, and other tests of a good camp site are satisfied. He knows in what direction to face the tents, how to measure out distances around camp, and how to map his camp site. He learns what wood to pick for fires and how to make camp furnishings using axe and rope.

Camp Cookery

Cooking in camp is quite different from hike cookery. On a hike, it is a matter of making a quick meal, eating it virtually "on the run." In camp, complete meals are required. The First Class Scout learns to plan and prepare a complete breakfast of fruit, cereals, bacon-and-eggs or pancakes for himself and at least one other companion; and a complete dinner of meat or fish or poultry, with at least one vegetable, dessert, and bread or biscuits or twist baked on a stick. In addition, the First Class Scout knows about edible wild greens, roots and fruits.

Signaling

Another test of a Boy Scout's preparedness is his ability to send a message by Morse signaling in case of an emergency. The most common Scout way of getting a message through is with the help of signal flags, "wigwagging" them from side to side to make the "dot"s and "dash"es (or "dit"s and "dah"s) of the Morse code letters. But there are other methods that Scouts can use: sending the letters by long and short flashes of a flashlight or other light source, by long and short sounds of whistle, bugle, or automobile horn—or even by short-wave radio.

First Aid

The first aid that a Scout learned to become Second Class is sufficient to make him able to take care of himself and others in simple accidents at home or in the open. The first aid for First Class is more advanced. It involves the use of the triangular Scout neckerchief as a bandage for wounds, and the care of fractures, puncture wounds, heat exhaustion, sunstroke, and frostbite. In addition, the First Class Scout must know under what circumstances an injured person should or should not be moved, and be able to arrange the transport of an accident victim if necessary.

Swimming

To "Be Prepared" a Boy Scout must be able to swim—not just for the sake of taking care of himself, but also so that he can come to the aid of people who may get into trouble in the water. For these reasons swimming is an important First Class test. The boy is required to know what precautions must be taken for a safe swim and must demonstrate his swimming ability. To pass the test, he must jump into deep water feet first and swim fifty yards—stopping part way through the swim, making a sharp turn, leveling off and resuming swimming.

THE CAMPING DAY has been wonderfully rich with explorations, games and contests, swimming and diving, opportunities for learning new outdoor skills that will make future camps even better.

Now the hustle and bustle of the day have ended. The shadows of night have fallen among the trees.

The boys have gathered in the campfire circle, and in their midst the fire bursts into flaming glory. The light flickers over the young, eager faces.

The campfire of the small patrol requires no formal program—song follows song as the spirit moves, the boys talk of the day's adventures and of the things that are ahead tomorrow. The campfire of the larger troop starts with a simple ceremony and moves through a program of group singing, solos, and patrol stunts. It has its boisterous moments of hilarity, and its quiet minutes when the boys gaze silently into the glowing embers while listening to their Scoutmaster telling them a story of courage and adventure.

To a Boy Scout camper, no other period of the camping day means as much as the evening's campfire.

It is here around the campfire that the boy feels the heart beat of the camp, and comes closest to understanding the ideals of Scouting.

CAMPFIRE MAGIC

CAMPOREE

THE BOY WHO JOINS an active patrol in a good troop will have plenty of excitement and fun ahead of him in the regular activities of his gang and his group. But there is still more Scouting adventure in store for him in large scale activities on a local, national and international level.

One of the most popular events in the Scouting year is the camporee, held on a district or council basis throughout the country, usually in the spring. The true camporee is a patrol event of a more or less competitive character. The patrols arrive under their own leadership, set up camp, build patrol kitchens, cook their own meals, and take part in a number of Scoutcraft contests to prove their ability. The camporee is an out-and-out outdoor experience, often with a campfire climax in which all patrols take part.

SCOUT-O-RAMA

THE SCOUT-O-RAMA, on the other hand, is generally an indoor event, staged in a large gymnasium, an armory, a convention hall—or in a place such as Madison Square Garden. Sometimes the Scout-o-rama takes the form of a merit badge show, with troops putting on live demonstrations of various merit badge subjects. At other times, the Scout-o-rama may be a Scout show, with Indians going in for pageantry and ceremonies, pioneers constructing rustic bridges and signal towers, Scouts pitching complete camps or demonstrating disaster service. The Scout-o-rama keeps the Scouts busy for months in advance with preparations that often result in the earning of scores of merit badges in the subject the troop has chosen.

JAMBOREE

IN A JAMBOREE, selected Scouts from every state of the United States or from every country in which Scouting is found gather in one tremendous friendship camp of up to fifty thousand campers. During the fifty years of the existence of the Boy Scouts of America, American Scouts have taken part in world jamborees in England, Denmark, Hungary, Holland, France, Canada, Austria, and the Philippines. In addition, America has had four national jamborees of its own.

A jamboree is a climactic event in the life of any Scout who is fortunate enough to take part. Here, more than anywhere else, he senses the magnitude of the movement of which he is a member—he makes friends with Scouts from other lands and learns the universal appeal of the Scout ideals to boys of good will—regardless of country, color and creed.

BE PREPARED *by Norman Rockwell*

MERIT BADGES

THE MERIT BADGE PROGRAM is one of the distinguishing features of Scouting. It challenges the Scout to try his hands in any one of a hundred different fields of endeavor and to earn recognition for his efforts in the form of colorful, embroidered badges.

From the boy's point of view the merit badge program gives him the opportunity to increase his skills in things he likes to do and to test new activities that may result in new interests.

From the point of view of parents and Scout leaders, the merit badge program is of even greater significance: It is the means of keeping older Scouts' interest alive; it prepares the boy for advanced service to his fellow man and to his community; it gives him an opportunity for vocational and avocational exploration; it brings him into personal contact with some of the finest men of his city or town who serve as merit badge counselors. The pursuit of merit badge skills aids the boy in discovering his native aptitudes and develops character through application, thoroughness, resourcefulness and service.

The success of the merit badge program is best proved by the fact that, over the fifty years of Boy Scouting, more than twenty-five million merit badges have been earned.

It is interesting to note that out of this great number, the merit badges that stand for service to others lead the rest: more than one million each of First Aid, Firemanship, and Public Health merit badges have been awarded, almost a million Safety merit badges, and close to three-quarter million Lifesaving merit badges.

Scoutcraft skills come next, with 650,000 Pioneering merit badges earned, 700,000 Camping, 1,100,000 Cooking, and 1,300,000 Swimming merit badges.

Scholastic learning ranks high, with more than half a million merit badges awarded in Scholarship and in Reading.

The remaining merit badges were earned mainly in the field of hobbies—ranging from Woodcarving to Indian Lore, from Leathercraft to Stamp Collecting; and in vocational exploration—running the gamut from Agriculture to Salesmanship, from Chemistry to Masonry.

One of the incentives for a Scout's progress in merit badge advancement is the fact that the mastery of certain numbers of them makes him eligible for advancement in rank to Star Scout and Life Scout and eventually to the rank a Scout covets the most—that of Eagle Scout. In the Eagle Scout rank is expressed the ideal toward which every Scout should aim—to be trained to a full degree in woodcraft and campcraft,

accustomed to service to his community, and thoroughly prepared to meet the emergencies of his everyday life.

For each of these advanced ranks—Star, Life, and Eagle—the boy must again demonstrate his growth in the three important phases of Scout advancement: SCOUT TEAMWORK, SCOUTCRAFT, SCOUT SPIRIT.

In Scout Teamwork, the emphasis now is on the development of latent leadership ability. Instead of participating in activities planned and run by others, the Scout aiming for Eagle rank is expected to step to the fore, volunteering his services, accepting leadership responsibility.

In Scoutcraft the boy working for Star Scout rank must earn five merit badges, for Life, ten, and for Eagle, twenty-one. For Star, the merit badges are pretty well of the boy's own choosing, but for the rank of Eagle, he is required to have earned specified merit badges in the fields of citizenship and public service, in outdoor skills and personal development.

In Scout Spirit, the higher rank requirements are increasingly demanding. Here, in addition to the testimony given by the boy's patrol and troop leaders of his efforts to live up to the Scout Oath and Law, evidence is also required from his parents, his teachers, his religious leaders, and from other people in the community who know the boy.

In spite of these high standards, close to one and a half million Star Scout badges, more than 600,000 Life Scout badges, and more than 350,000 Eagle Scout badges have been awarded in the years since 1910.

STAR—LIFE—
AND EAGLE

Pro Deo et Patria
(Lutheran)

God and Country
(Episcopal)

Ner Tamid
(Jewish)

God and Country
(Protestant)

Alpha Omega
(Eastern Orthodox)

Ad Altare Dei
(Roman Catholic)

Duty to God
(Mormon)

Sangha
(Buddhist)

RELIGIOUS
AWARDS

Among special awards available to Boy Scouts, four rank especially high: the religious award, the conservation award, the Medal of Merit, and the Gold Honor Medal.

ALL SCOUTS are expected to be faithful in their religious duties. The importance of Scouting in a boy's spiritual growth has been recognized by most religious leaders and the major religious denominations have created special awards for First Class Scouts who do outstanding service within their faiths.

The first of these awards was the *Ad Altare Dei* award established by the Roman Catholic Church in 1931. This was followed in quick succession by the *God and Country* award for Scouts of the Protestant faiths, the Lutheran *Pro Deo et Patria* award, *Ner Tamid* for Scouts of the Jewish faith, the *Duty to God* award for Scouts of the Church of Jesus Christ of Latter-Day Saints, the *Sangha* award for Scouts who are Buddhists, the *Alpha Omega* award for Scouts of the Eastern Orthodox Catholic Church, and the *God and Country* award of the Episcopal Church.

FROM ITS INCEPTION, the Boy Scouts of America has been active in the field of conservation—one of its earliest merit badges was a badge in Conservation. In 1914 the Scout movement further established the William T. Hornaday Award for Distinguished Service to Conservation. It is named for the first director of the New York Zoological Society—one of the staunchest pioneers for conservation in our nation's history.

There are no specific requirements for this award, but the work done must add up to "Distinguished Service" in the field of conservation.

A SCOUT who performs some outstanding act of service, putting into practice the ideals and skills of Scouting without necessarily risking his life, may be awarded a medal of merit by the National Court of Honor of the Boy Scouts of America.

Such medals have been awarded for exceptional first aid, for swimming and boating rescues, and for service in hurricanes and floods and other emergencies.

THE HIGHEST special award in Scouting is the Gold Honor Medal. This is awarded by the National Court of Honor to Scouts who save life or attempt to save life at the risk of their own and show heroism, resourcefulness and skill.

The earliest Boy Scout honor medals, awarded in 1910, consisted of a bronze cross "for saving life at risk of own" and a silver cross "for saving life or helping to save life without risk to self." These were superceded, in 1911, by three medals—bronze "for saving life," silver "for saving life with considerable risk to himself," gold "for saving life at greatest possible risk to his own life." As more and more lives were saved, it became increasingly difficult to determine the exact degree of risk in each case. For this reason, the National Court of Honor, in 1922, settled on a single medal of gold, to be awarded in cases of great heroism. This medal was designed by the prominent artist Belmore Browne.

The files of the National Court of Honor contain an inspiring record of Scouts who have saved the lives of their fellow men under the most hazardous conditions—from drownings in oceans and rivers and lakes, from fires and other disasters. The deed for which Gold Honor Medals have been awarded have been mostly performed by boys in their teens who, forgetful of self, have acted with courage and cool-headed resolve when the emergency struck.

MEDAL OF MERIT

GOLD HONOR MEDAL

Medal of Merit 1910

Bronze and Silver Cross for saving life 1910

Present Honor Medal

Scouting for Older Boys

A PROGRAM that wasn't so intended became the first "older boy" program of the Boy Scouts of America.

When *Scouting for Boys* appeared in book form in May, 1908, Baden-Powell had included in it a short "campfire yarn" in which he impressed his boy readers with the importance of the ability to swim and to handle a boat. In this "yarn" he explained the things that sailors and Scouts have in common and added:

"I hope that there are many Boy Scouts who, by taking up 'sea scouting,' and by learning boat management and seamanship, will be able to take their place in the service of their country as seamen on our battleships or in our great merchant service, or as lifeboatmen upon our coasts."

This quite casual remark soon resulted in a clamor raised by boys interested in the sea. They wanted to know more about "sea scouting" and what Sea Scouts were supposed to do.

Baden-Powell used the summer of 1909 to look further into the matter. He ran another training camp along the lines of the famous Brownsea Island camp near the historic village of Buckler's Hard, Hampshire, England, on land that had been the site of the ancient slipways from which many of Lord Nelson's ships were launched. Two troops of Scouts took part

A Sea Scout— from a drawing by Baden-Powell

in this experience, alternating between land and sea Scouting—spending part of the time ashore in camp and part of it aboard a training ship, the "Mercury," placed at Baden-Powell's disposal by its owner. The outcome was a decision to establish Sea Scouting as a branch of the British Boy Scouts.

"The idea of Sea Scouts," the official "Scout Gazette" proclaimed in announcing the new program early in 1910, "is to sound the call of the sea in the ears of boys of our cities and seaports, and to give them an elementary training which may be useful, whether in starting them on a seaman's career or in making them handy men for any branch of life."

For the writing of a suitable handbook on seamanship, Baden-Powell turned to his older brother, Warington, who had been his boyhood "captain" on boat trips of the Baden-Powell brothers up and down the Thames and Avon rivers and on sailing cruises on the North Sea and in the English Channel. Warington's book, *Sea Scouting for Boys*, appeared in 1912 and was enthusiastically received by Britain's sea-minded youngsters.

The same Scouting "call of the sea" sounded across the Atlantic Ocean in the ears of a New England sailing enthusiast and member of the National Council of the Boy Scouts of America—Arthur A. Carey, of Waltham, Massachusetts.

Carey had already helped prepare a chapter for the first American Boy Scout handbook on "canoeing, rowing, and sailing," based on his experiences as "Scout Master" of the "Boy Scoutship 'Pioneer'." Now he developed his experiences in organizing and running a ship of Sea Scouts into a 24-page pamphlet, *Cruising for Sea Scouts*—the first American Sea Scout "handbook."

In this pamphlet, Sea Scouts were defined as being of two classes:

"Landsmen are boys between twelve and fourteen years old who attend the meetings and classes of the Sea Scouts ashore, but are not allowed to take part in the summer cruises.

"Apprentice Seamen are boys of fourteen years or older, and their age gives them the opportunity of cruising in the summer."

It was just as impossible for boys of twelve, in the year 1912, to "hang around" for two years waiting for a taste of the "real thing" as it would be for twelve-year olds today. The obvious result was that mostly older boys joined up.

A national committee was established to look into the advisability of formally creating a Sea Scout branch of the Boy

Sea Scout uniforms 1912

Scouts of America. The committee reported favorably on the subject and recommended that assistance be sought from the U. S. Navy Department in matters pertaining to seamanship. This help was readily forthcoming when the Secretary of the Navy, G. V. L. Meyer, in a general order of February 27, 1913, authorized navy personnel to co-operate in every way possible with the Boy Scouts of America.

In the years that followed, Sea Scouting spread slowly—first along the Atlantic and Pacific seacoasts, then inland.

But in 1917, two events caused a rapid spurt in the Sea Scout membership.

The first of these was the entrance of the United States into the first World War. This created a sudden, tremendous interest in nautical activities among boys and thousands of youngsters became Sea Scouts and put on the "snappy" (in those days) uniform of "khaki jumper with blue drill cuffs and collar, regulation sailor breeches with bellspringed bottoms, sailor's cravat and dark blue lanyard, and cap in plain khaki."

The second event was the appearance on the scene of "Kimo"—James Austin Wilder, of Hawaii, veteran sailor, wealthy globe traveler, artist, colorful figure, and tireless worker in Scouting.

Wilder approached the Chief Scout Executive, James E. West, insisting that if Sea Scouting were to prosper, a separate

Sea Scouting founded 1912

department of the National Office must be established, with full-time personnel to promote the program.

West readily agreed to this need.

"But who will do the job?" he asked. "I will!" said Wilder.

"And who will pay the salaries?" West asked. "I will!" said Wilder.

Wilder went to work with the title of Chief Seascout.

The Sea Scout department was established and a pamphlet was rushed into print explaining the aims and scope of Sea Scouting, with a summary of new program features, insignia and equipment. At the same time, the requirements for joining were set at "First Class, 115 pounds, and over fourteen" with "good eyes, good muscles, good heart" and parental permission.

Sea Scouting had become the older boy program of the Boy Scouts of America—soon after with a complete handbook of its own, the *Seascout Manual*, in which the age requirement was raised to fifteen and the weight lowered to 112 pounds.

For a number of years, Sea Scouting was the only older boy program conducted by the Boy Scouts of America. But as time passed it became more and more evident that a program concentrating exclusively on the activities of the sea was not sufficient to attract and hold all older boys.

A study of the problem, made possible by a Laura Spelman

Exploring founded 1935

Air Scouting founded 1941

Rockefeller Memorial grant in 1927, expressed the hope that "the search for the *one* perfect universally-appealing 'older boy' or 'young man' program might cease. The fact of individual differences, and the fact that these diverged yet more at the ages above 15, narrowed the search (or widened it perhaps) to seek the best types of older boy programs from which selections might be made by the local community."

In 1935, the Sea Scouting Service of the National Office became the Senior Scouting Service, and the boy was given the choice among several courses he could take on reaching fifteen: to remain in his Boy Scout troop as a Senior Scout, to become a Sea Scout or an Explorer Scout. His choice was further increased in 1941 when, as the result of the interest in aviation engendered by the second World War, the Boy Scouts of America established Air Scouting as still another branch of its program for older boys. In this work, the Scout movement received the same generous co-operation from the U. S. Air Force as Sea Scouting had received from the U. S. Navy and Explorer Scouting from the U. S. Army.

The fifteen-year requirement continued in force until 1949 when the National Executive Board, in an over-all revision in the Senior Scout program, recognized all young men in Scouting fourteen years of age and over as Explorers—whether in Boy Scout troops or in special Explorer units.

The years following World War II profoundly affected the thinking and interests of the mid-adolescent American boy. It became imperative for the Boy Scouts of America to find out, by a thorough, scientific evaluation, to what extent the Exploring program suited the modern boy and what changes were needed to make it more acceptable and more effective. Such a study was undertaken by the Research Service of the National Office and the Survey Research Center of the Institute for Social Research at the University of Michigan.

As the result of this study, a modernized Exploring program went into effect in 1959. Its main feature was a wide variety of activities intended to appeal to all young men, whether or not they had been Boy Scouts. Sea and Air Exploring remained unchanged, but for all phases of Exploring the age requirement was placed at "fourteen and in the ninth grade or higher, or fifteen regardless of grade."

The new Exploring program found ready acceptance throughout the country and quickly proved itself a major forward step in providing the youth of America with high-interest activities and forward-looking ideals.

CARRY ON *by Norman Rockwell*

SENIOR SCOUTING

TODAY'S EXPLORING

EXPLORER POST STRUCTURE AND LEADERSHIP

ACTION AND EXPLORING are synonymous. In the Exploring program, young men organize themselves into companionable groups called "posts," for the purpose of planning and participating in meaningful activities that will carry them onward into strong and dedicated citizenship.

There are no spectators in the Explorer post—every member is an active participant in everything that happens. Some of the Explorers are elected into office and assume leadership responsibilities as president, vice president, secretary, treasurer, quartermaster, or cabinet representative. These elected officers, with all the rest, make up activity committees that work out the details of activities decided upon and conduct the projects according to plan

This organizational structure has only one basic aim—not just to give titles to some Explorers, not just to set up neat routines to follow—but to help the post plan and run the best possible program.

Behind each post stands a post committee of three or more men appointed by the institution that sponsors the post. This committee secures the services of several adults to guide the work. The key man among these officers is the Advisor who keeps the post moving on the right course. He is assisted by one or more associate Advisors, and calls in consultants whenever a scheduled activity requires technical skill.

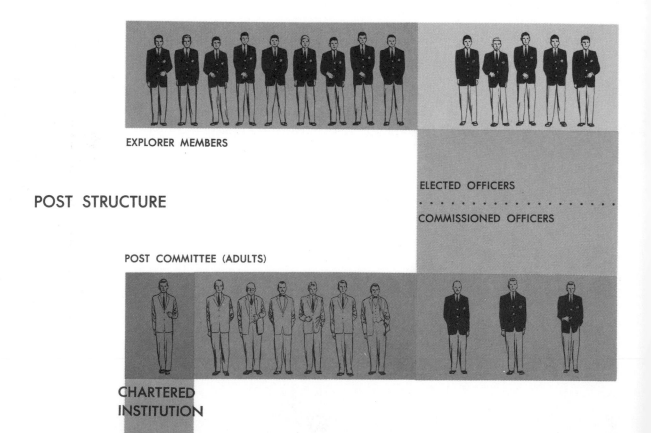

EXPLORER MEMBERS

ELECTED OFFICERS

COMMISSIONED OFFICERS

POST STRUCTURE

POST COMMITTEE (ADULTS)

CHARTERED INSTITUTION

Social experiences

Vocational experiences

Personal fitness experiences

Outdoor experiences

Service experiences

Citizenship experiences

THE EXPLORING STUDY conducted in 1955 by the Research Service of the Boy Scouts of America and the University of Michigan set out to ascertain exactly what activities the American high school boy wanted to do, liked to do, and felt that he needed to do.

Out of this nationwide survey came a listing of a great mass of activities—but also the clear-cut revelation that teen-age boys realize that a balance of experiences in many different fields is required to develop them into well-rounded young men.

This "balance of experiences" is provided through regular post activities, specialties, and "superactivities" in the six experience areas that make up the Exploring program:

Vocational experiences to provide opportunities for exploration into various skills and occupations.

Social experiences to improve the Explorers' ability to get along with other people—friends, strangers, adults, girls.

Outdoor experiences for adventure and recreation.

Personal fitness experiences to help in the development of self-reliance through physical, mental and emotional growth.

Service experiences to furnish occasions for helping other people and for taking on unselfish leadership responsibilities.

Citizenship experiences to give a clear understanding of American democracy and the rights and duties of a citizen.

PROGRAM AREAS
OF EXPLORING

THE EXPLORER CODE

AS AN EXPLORER—

I believe that America's strength lies in her trust in God and in the courage and strength of her people.

I will, therefore, be faithful in my religious duties and will maintain a personal sense of honor in my own life.

I will treasure my American heritage and will do all I can to preserve and enrich it.

I will recognize the dignity and worth of my fellow men and will use fair play and good will in dealing with them.

I will acquire the Exploring attitude that seeks the truth in all things and adventure on the frontiers of our changing world.

THE EXPLORER MOTTO

**OUR BEST TODAY—
FOR A BETTER TOMORROW**

THE EXPLORER SALUTE

THE EXPLORER EMBLEM

The Explorer emblem gives the general impression of movement and speed—directed movement and controlled speed. The design is dynamic—suggesting that Exploring is dynamic, creative, forward-looking, modern.

The "V" in the center is symbolic of the Explorer's growth and progress. It is formed by two prisms representing his duty to self and duty to his fellow men. As they merge, they point into infinity—symbolic of his duty to God.

The circles represent the Explorer's environment—his home, school, community, and nation. The colors of the circles remind him of his American heritage.

The traditional fleur-de-lis stands for the Explorer's affiliation with the Boy Scouts of America and the world brotherhood of Scouting.

THE EXPLORER UNIFORM

The green Explorer uniform is the perfect outfit for many activities; it has the rugged stamina that makes it ideal for wilderness adventuring.

For other activities, the optional Explorer outfit sets the pace for the program. Campus-styled blue blazer with emblem, gray slacks, white shirt, and maroon tie make an attractive combination that suits the taste of a teen-ager for all dress-up occasions: socials, community events, conferences.

POST ACTIVITIES

EXPLORERS get together for post meetings at least twice a month. These meetings generally include a short business session—but most of the time is used for the special activity of the month.

In the summer time, such an activity may be a splash party in a local swimming pool, a visit to a children's hospital to entertain a group of young patients, a Saturday at a rifle range or golf course. In the winter, the looked-forward-to event may be a co-ed dinner-dance, attendance at a town-council meeting, safety service at the municipal skating pond.

POST SUPER-ACTIVITIES

MOST ACTIVE Explorer posts schedule a superactivity during the year. To be considered "super," the activity must entail high adventure—the challenge of a new experience.

To an Explorer post in the country, a big-city sightseeing tour may be "super." To a city post, the "super" designation would fit a week's cruise by canoe through some wilderness area, a back-packing trek or a horseback trip along mountain trails. To Explorers everywhere, the "super-super" of all super-activities is participation in a Philmont expedition or a visit to a foreign country.

A POST SPECIALTY is a special pursuit that appeals to the majority of the Explorers. It may keep the post busy for a month or a year—or be a continuous theme such as seamanship among Sea Explorers and aerodynamics among Air Explorers.

In an industrial location, an Explorer post may secure laboratory training in chemistry or electronics. In a town with an active rescue squad, the Explorers may take up first aid training and emergency service. A post with literary interests may establish a discussion group on current books; a theatrically inclined post may stage a play, a musically inclined post put on a concert.

POST
SPECIALTIES

VOCATIONAL EXPERIENCES

EVERY DAY that passes brings the Explorer closer to the problem of selecting his life work. He looks out on a world in turmoil, spinning at jet speed, and knows that, before long, he must take his place in it to make his contribution to it while providing for his own survival. He realizes more and more that whatever he will amount to in the future depends on the decisions he makes today, that his educational plans of the moment must be consistent with his job aspirations as an adult.

Question upon question clamor for an answer.

"What life work should I pick? What job am I best suited for? What education do I need for it? Should I go to work or continue my education after high school? What about military service? Should I wait to be drafted or should I enlist?"

The boy in Exploring has a unique opportunity for vocational exploration. The program and the purpose of the Boy Scouts of America have always had a remarkable appeal to men of high caliber. In every community, the Boy Scout council has attracted the services of top men in all branches of endeavor. These men are not only willing but eager to help when called upon. Utilizing such men, many Explorer posts arrange regular program features in vocational exploration.

Such a feature may take the form of a "career parade" at which a group of men take turns briefly describing their own occupations and answering the Explorers' questions about them. Or the program may spotlight a specific career field—science, teaching, engineering—with personnel directors, educators, and other men working in the field explaining the opportunities in it and the required qualifications.

Similarly, information in regard to military service may readily be provided in a post activity. A "military service preview" for sons and dads does the job effectively—with a member of the draft board or of a veterans' organization, or members of the different branches of the service on hand to explain and discuss what is involved.

The Explorers can supplement this exploration for the future in discussions among themselves. To do this successfully, individual Explorers investigate certain specific vocations more fully and present their findings to the whole post. Even a small group of Explorers, by agreement among themselves, can cover a number of occupations in this manner.

In addition to these "bull sessions," an Explorer post may turn its vocational investigation into a special activity—a visit to a manufacturing plant, a wholesale house, a bank, a department store, a laboratory, a farm, a military base, for the purpose of observing and securing first-hand information.

THE SOCIAL EXPERIENCES of Exploring are far more than occasions for pleasure and recreation and "boy-meets-girl" get-togethers. Of far greater value is the opportunity that each occasion provides for teaching the young man correct social observances and behavior and helping him feel at home in social matters.

SOCIAL EXPERIENCES

No young man likes to appear awkward in a social setting. He wants to be able to associate with other people with ease and natural poise, to possess the good manners that are the outward signs of a gentleman. He wants to fit into the pattern of his own society. He soon discovers that helping to organize and participating in Explorer socials cause him to put manners into practice and to act the part of a gentleman as well as being one at heart. He also learns that good manners and good taste are not limitations to intelligent people—on the contrary, they are an insurance of good times, the kind that are fun while you're having them and remain fun as long as you remember them.

There are many sorts of affairs to which the Explorers of a post may want to invite their young lady friends. These occasions will vary with the traditions of the community and the social and recreational usages of the sponsoring institution.

Most of these socials will be informal—splash parties at the beach, fireside wiener roasts, pot-luck suppers to which each person brings a dish, barn dances, sleigh rides, house parties or game evenings. Others will be formal, with the girls dressing up and the boys getting into their blazer outfits for a dinner dance, a St. Valentine's or other holiday party, a progressive dinner, a theatre or concert party for post members and guests, a district or local council Explorer ball or award ceremony, a party for the sponsoring institution or for some visiting honored guest or dignitary.

Socials are not necessarily one-shot activities. A post may, for example, decide to take up dramatics—for the sheer fun of it, or for entertainment at a district or council event, or for the purpose of earning money for the sponsoring institution. For such an experience, many roles may be assigned to young ladies—not just dramatic parts, but also the designing of scenery and costumes, and handling the details of "getting the show on the road."

There are many different types of socials—not all of them are co-ed.

A big annual event in the well-run post is "charter night" when the post receives its charter for the coming year. Father-and-son dinners are recurring occasions in many Explorer posts. So are "open houses" where friends of the post have a chance to come visiting to view special demonstrations, exhibits, and ceremonies.

In many Explorer posts, major social events are held at intervals of a couple of months—all carefully worked out.

Generally, the post as a whole decides on a theme or central idea for the social and turns the job of planning and running it over to an activity committee under a capable chairman. It then becomes the responsibility of the Explorers chosen for the committee to look after all the details of physical arrangements, to find the right place for holding the event, and to have the right men and the right materials on hand at the right time. In the case of a formal occasion, this may involve securing a hall, invitations and tickets, music or other entertainment, decorations and favors, enough refreshments to satisfy everyone, dishes and silverware, hosts and chaperons —and numerous other details.

The caliber of the people in Exploring and the nature of the ideals underlying the program unite to set a high level of good tone in all the social affairs of an Explorer post. The Explorers themselves have matured to the age of young manhood and therefore have graduated from the sometimes kiddish kind of gathering of their younger days. They want their social affairs to run smoothly and to be big occasions giving complete satisfaction to all participants.

OUTDOOR EXPERIENCES

THE VERY WORD "Exploring" suggests rugged adventure in the open. An Explorer does not abandon a planned expedition to the summit of a mountain because there is no trail—he maps out and cuts his own trail if necessary.

It is not unusual for an Explorer post to schedule three or four expeditions a year—at least one of them a "superactivity."

The smaller expeditions may be day trips only or may be overnight.

When the trout season opens, for instance, the whole post may take off on a fishing trip, camping over a weekend or staying at a fishing lodge for a couple of days.

Another post may become interested in learning the skills required for traveling cross-country with map and compass and may wind up its training with a tough orienteering race through rough territory.

A cave in a nearby mountain range may lure an Explorer post to secure an expert guide for a day's adventure of "spelunking" underground. A large body of water within easy reach may provide another post with an opportunity for a cruise on a power or sail boat.

In addition to the shorter expeditions, many Explorer posts have a major expedition during the year, with the whole gang setting out on a trip lasting as long as vacation and money permit. This week or two on the trail with horses, bikes, cars, or on foot, or on the water with paddles, sail, or motor, usually becomes the highlight of the Exploring year.

Such a major expedition does not start with the trip itself; it starts back in civilization long before the date set for the take-off. It starts with careful planning, with detailed study of the areas to be explored, with maps and routes, equipment lists, advice from experts, reading, practicing, body toughening, and the careful selection or making of the proper equipment—with every Explorer in the act, taking on and carrying out a responsibility important to the success of the undertaking.

On these expeditions, it becomes not just a matter of seeing things but also of understanding what is seen—the country, its natural resources, its history.

Traveling by canoe is a thrilling experience in itself—but it takes on added significance to the Explorer who thinks of the rivers he follows and the lakes he crosses as being America's original highways—over them went the explorers and discoverers who opened up the great American continent.

Other major expeditions have similar objectives beyond the traveling itself.

Explorers have followed the Pacific Crest Trail in the West, from the borders of Canada to the borders of Mexico, and the Appalachian Trail in the East that stretches from the peak of mighty Mount Kathadin in Maine to Mount Oglethorpe in Georgia, and have helped to break and mark many miles of trails.

Explorers have traversed Western mountain ridges on horseback and have crisscrossed the New England states on foot. They have traveled into foreign countries and have made friends for themselves and for our own country.

On all of these expeditions they have had adventure and fun and comradeship, but also the opportunity of learning the skills of the outdoorsman, of toughening their bodies, of getting a new appreciation of their own country and of countries abroad.

107

PERSONAL FITNESS EXPERIENCES

WHEN SPEAKING of personal fitness, there has been a tendency to think mostly of *physical* fitness—well-developed muscles and bodily strength.

In Exploring it is realized that muscular development is only part of the picture, that complete fitness involves the whole person—his body, his mind, and his spirit. Physical fitness is important—but so is mental and emotional, moral and spiritual fitness, if a person is to be considered truly fit, equal to the demands of life.

The desperate need for the future is for youth that is fit—physically, mentally, morally.

Exploring strives to create in youth a desire for such personal fitness as a vital part of preparing for their own happiness and for their usefulness to others in the days ahead. It provides for its development in all its aspects through a program of personal fitness experiences.

Physical fitness is stressed in sports and outdoor activities.

The individual Explorer may be encouraged to take up track and field, fly and bait casting, hunting, golf, swimming, ice skating, or some other sport of a personal nature. Or the Explorer may join up with a buddy and go in for fencing or wrestling, skin diving or tennis or some other two-person sport.

As a special activity for the whole post, the Explorers may decide on riflery or orienteering, or on some indoor or outdoor team sport. Camping and canoeing, hiking and bicycling may become the basis for a post "superactivity."

All of these activities, sponsored by an Explorer post, start with a medical examination of the members so that each boy will know the condition of his body and can build on this knowledge. This examination is followed by a period of training and

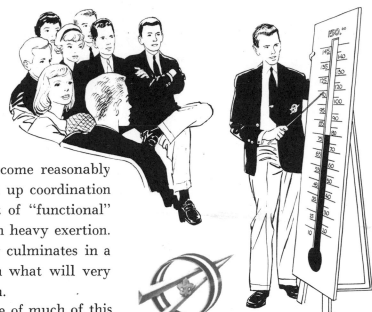

conditioning during which the Explorers become reasonably skilled in the subject they have chosen, pick up coordination and muscular strength, and reach the point of "functional" fitness where they recover quickly, even from heavy exertion. In the case of a "superactivity," the training culminates in a shakedown even before the post starts off on what will very likely be the highlight of the year's program.

Mental and emotional fitness is an outcome of much of this training. Many of the activities require concentration and learning, adjustment and study, planning and scheduling. Most of them demand the skill of getting along with other people, considering their feelings, learning the give-and-take of human relationships. The activities bring out sportsmanship and fair play and the ability to take what comes in a good spirit— whether it is losing a game, having a trip rained out, or dropping the supplies in "the drink" when a canoe upsets.

Numerous other Explorer activities assist in the development of an alert, disciplined, and trained mind. The planning session of the regular post meeting forces each Explorer to "say his piece," to judge, to participate in making decisions. He learns proper parliamentary procedure, learns to express himself on behalf of his committee. When mingling with outstanding men of his community at some post activity, he develops the arts of being at ease, of listening and adding to his knowledge.

In Exploring, the ideals of the Scout Oath and Law, and the high resolve of the Explorer Code to which the young man has pledged himself are always at work—moral and spiritual fitness is continuously building.

There is no preaching or moralizing in Exploring. The work that goes on in the post month-in-and-month-out helps to instill in each Explorer the spirit of loyalty, helpfulness, and unselfishness. In trying to live up to his obligations and the high standards he has set for himself the Explorer develops the ingredients of a strong character and makes himself fit for the future—not only for his chosen profession but as a husband and father of tomorrow.

SERVICE EXPERIENCES

THE SPIRIT of today's Explorer service is the same as the pioneers' spirit of neighborliness in the past, at barn raisings and husking bees. It is the idea of "All for One—One for All" put into practice.

To an Explorer, service means giving or doing something for other people without expecting a return. The Explorer, being older, is capable of more sustained and more adult responsibilities than the Boy Scout. Because of his added years and experiences, people naturally expect more of him in his service work.

The members of an Explorer post, by working together, are capable of undertaking more ambitious service projects than a single individual can manage—to the institution that sponsors the post, to the local council of which the post is a part, and to the community in which it functions.

To the sponsoring institution—church or synagogue, school or club—the service performed by Explorers may take the form of a major overhaul of the sponsor's property—repairing and painting the buildings, leveling and planting the grounds. Or the service may involve week-in-week-out assistance in the activities of the institution—ushering, helping in a parking lot, caring for lawns and other areas, conducting certain activities.

In almost every local Boy Scout council in the country many

Explorers take on the responsibility of leadership in Scout units, and act as instructors, camporee judges, camp counselors, training course aides, and in numerous other capacities.

The service of Explorers to the community as a whole is a matter of close co-operation between the posts and the local authorities. Explorers have been active in community clean-up efforts, as convention guides, in traffic studies, in Civil Defense work, and have co-operated with county officials in various conservation efforts. In times of disaster—floods, explosions, fires, tornadoes, and hurricanes—Explorers are generally called out to render special service.

For this kind of service, preparedness is of the greatest importance. Knowing this, many Explorer posts have organized themselves into emergency service groups with an extensive training program in the four fields in which experience has shown that young men of Explorer age are qualified to be of the greatest help:

Light-duty rescue work—making use of first aid, firemanship, and lifesaving knowledge.

Communications—sending and receiving messages by telephone or radio, carrying messages by bicycle, boat, auto, and on foot.

Public safety—clearing away light debris with hand tools, guiding traffic, posting and guarding hazardous areas.

Emergency living—providing and improvising emergency shelter, food, and clothing for disaster-struck families.

CITIZENSHIP EXPERIENCES

ALL THE OTHER five Explorer experience areas—vocational, social, outdoors, personal fitness, and service—lend emphasis to the area of citizenship. They are roads that lead the young man to be a more competent participating citizen here and now, better trained for the voting citizenship that will shortly be his.

In vocational experiences, the Explorer has a chance to investigate many fields of endeavor, to explore, to check and countercheck, to discover by listening and looking and deducing what life work he is best qualified for.

In social experiences, he learns to get along with other people, finds out the importance of careful planning and executing in making an activity successful.

In outdoor experiences, he becomes self-reliant, able to survive under wilderness conditions, able to accept "the bitter with the better"—the rain with the sun, the storm with the warm breeze, the "white water" of a turbulent river as a welcome change from the smoothness of a placid lake.

In personal fitness experiences, he builds his inner and outer self.

In service experiences, he learns to give of himself to help other people who need the support of a young arm, the uplift of a youthful spirit.

In all of these experiences, the Explorer comes to the realization that although citizenship may include such exciting deeds as piloting a jet plane from the deck of a Navy carrier in defense of his country, it is far more likely to revolve around such matter-of-fact actions as securing the necessary education to be a self-supporting, peace-building citizen, and co-operating well with other people. Whether he becomes a national or international leader or an ordinary citizen, the Explorer knows that the part he plays is as important as the next fellow's—that the peace of the world will last as long as enough individuals share in unselfish, well-thought-out doing rather than in idle thinking.

The Explorer learns that citizenship is not only his relationship to local and national government, but also his relationship to life itself. He knows that one can not be a good citizen and be a crooked merchant, one can not be a good citizen and be a bad husband and father, one can not be a good citizen and be self-centered and miserly. He learns to think of the "good citizen" as one who is well-adjusted personally and socially, and who seeks to contribute something to the various life areas in which he moves.

One of the most impressive experiences in the citizenship field in which an Explorer can take part is a "Citizens Now" conference. This is a large-scale gathering of all the Explorers of a district or a local council. It is planned and conducted by the Explorers themselves with adults as advisors and is held at some college or university.

The purpose of the "Citizens Now" conference is to focus the attention of the Explorers on the fact that there is no miracle age at which they suddenly leave the stage of preparation and become active citizens—they are citizens *now*.

The program of the conference is planned to show each Explorer that he has a Bill of Responsibilities to live up to, as well as a Bill of Rights to live under, in his home and his community.

The conference encourages the young men in their vocational aspirations by bringing them in contact with college or university atmosphere and leadership and by giving them the opportunity to meet and listen to outstanding leaders in business, industry, educational, religious, and social fields. But far more important, it gives them the chance to get together in small discussion groups under clear-thinking young discussion leaders—Explorers like themselves—to draw out each other, to find mutual answers to problems that bother them, to express themselves, to talk over their privileges and obligations within the family and in the community.

The young men leave a "Citizens Now" conference with a deep awareness of the importance of their American citizenship and the reaffirmed appreciation of being a part of a great, purposeful movement.

Volunteer Leaders

WHEN BADEN-POWELL made public his "Boy Scout Scheme" he had no intention of starting a new youth movement. His plan was mainly to present a number of activities of great boy interest which existing organizations might adopt and use to add to the attractiveness of their program.

In the very first installment of *Scouting for Boys* he told the boy reader, "To become a Boy Scout you join a patrol belonging to your Cadet Corps, or Boys' Brigade or club."

But Baden-Powell was well aware of the fact that such organizations did not exist throughout the United Kingdom. He therefore added:

"If you are not a member of one of these, or if it does not as yet possess a patrol of Scouts, you can raise a patrol yourself by getting five other boys to join. . . . Several patrols together can form a 'troop' under an officer called a 'Scoutmaster.'"

While many British boys' organizations instantly accepted Scouting as part of their program, a large number of boys preferred to band themselves together as Scouts, independent of existing organizations. This raised the all-important question of getting adult leadership of sufficiently high caliber to help the boys keep their Scouting on the right track.

Baden-Powell found adult leaders readily available. Within a few months, in September of 1908, he was able to say:

"To a very considerable extent this question (of leadership) was settled by the boys themselves. They had the sense to recognize that grown-up officers were necessary, and they went around among the men of their respective neighborhoods until they found those willing to become their leaders.

"I realized that there was in our population a considerable

**THE MAN
BEHIND
THE BOY**

*"Scouter's Key"
training award*

THE SCOUTMASTER *by Norman Rockwell*

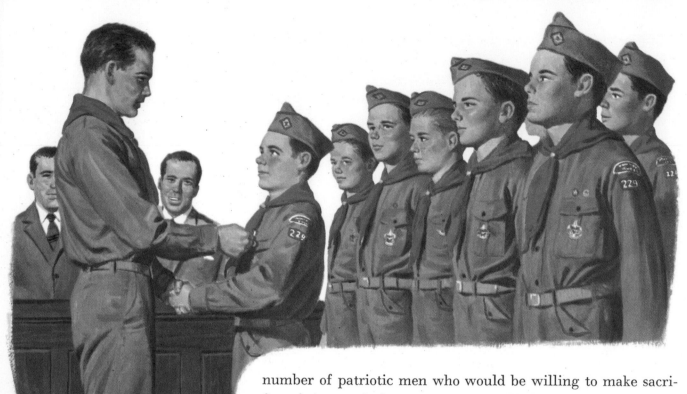

THE SCOUTMASTER

number of patriotic men who would be willing to make sacrifice of time and pleasure to come and take charge of the boys. But I never foresaw the amazing response which has been given by such men to the call of the Scout movement.

"To them is due the remarkable growth and results achieved."

Baden-Powell knew that willingness to serve was not sufficient qualification for Scoutmastership. He repeatedly emphasized that adult leaders in Scouting needed to understand that "the position of Scoutmaster is neither that of a schoolmaster nor of a commanding officer, but rather that of an elder brother *among* his boys—not detached or above them, but himself joining in their activities and sharing their enthusiasm, and thus, being in the position to know them individually, able to inspire their efforts."

The term "Scoutmaster," incidentally, was not of Baden-Powell's invention. It was an old English title which he, with his uncanny sense for always picking the word that was exactly right, chose for the name of the adult leader of a troop of Scouts. The title appears for the first time in print in 1579 in Leonard Digges' book *Stratioticos:* "The Scout maister oughte diligently to viewe and note aboute the campe." Oliver Cromwell had "Scoutmasters" in his Army, and Walter Scott, in *Ivanhoe*, had Prince John ordering his attendant, "Bid Barden our Scoutmaster come hither."

Baden-Powell further expounded his ideas about Scoutmastership in the columns of the British Scout leaders' magazine,

Headquarters Gazette, and finally wrote them out in the form of six sessions of a training course which a Scoutmaster could take by correspondence.

When James E. West, in January, 1911, assumed the executive leadership of the Boy Scouts of America, he was well aware of the problems that had arisen in England in the early days of Scouting and was determined to secure, from the beginning, the best possible volunteer leadership for the Scout troops in the United States.

It was freely predicted at that time that it would be impossible to get men to give continuous and sustained leadership unless they were paid for it—the idea of using volunteer leaders was something new in boys' work.

But West believed otherwise. He insisted "that leadership positions in Scouting, directly related to boys, be held by men who have volunteered their service—men who, because of their interest in boys and their enthusiasm for those principles and activities which constitute the program of Scouting, find therein a fascinating and constructive hobby." The years have proved the soundness of this viewpoint.

The selection of leaders and their training became two of West's most pressing functions.

During 1910, the number of men starting and operating troops had been so great that the small national staff had been incapable of keeping up with the process of commissioning them, and those who were commissioned were authorized for an indefinite period. Beginning with 1911, the commissions of all Scoutmasters were made for one year, renewable upon application and proper endorsement. This enabled the movement to insist upon each applicant establishing his fitness to serve as a leader of boys.

As far as training was concerned, West realized that the first need was to gather the experiences of successful Scoutmasters into a book and to make this available to all leaders. Such a book was prepared and sent in proof form, free of charge, to all Scoutmasters commissioned at the time, asking for their criticism and suggestions. The resulting *Handbook for Scoutmasters* was published in 1913.

Simultaneously, a leaders' magazine, SCOUTING, began its semi-monthly appearance for the purpose of providing Scoutmasters with inspiration and program ideas, and to get them into a "more harmonious relation with headquarters."

As a step in the direction of training all Scoutmasters in Scout methods and principles, SCOUTING magazine, from

Explorer Advisor

Merit Badge Counselor

Cubmaster

SCOUTMASTER TRAINING

Den Mother

September 15 to December 1, 1914, featured the entire series of Baden-Powell's "Scoutmasters' Training Course."

In the meantime, the idea of Scoutmasters' conferences and courses had spread across America.

The *Handbook for Scoutmasters* advocated that Scoutmasters in a community get together in bi-weekly or monthly conferences for the discussion of local problems and that "schools for Scoutmasters" be conducted so that each Scoutmaster might "learn of plans that have met with success in other troops and gain helpful suggestions about problems that confront him in the conduct of his own work."

The training work on a national basis began with summer schools and summer training camps conducted by national leaders. The earliest school of this kind was held at Silver Bay, New York, in the summer of 1910, with forty men present and with Ernest Thompson Seton, Dan Beard, and Edgar M. Robinson among the instructors.

Soon after, colleges and universities, realizing the educational values of Scouting, began to include it in their courses. That was the case at the universities of Virginia, Wisconsin, Texas, California, and at Cornell and Columbia.

While the National Council was giving a certain amount of "guidance" to these courses, there was no set curriculum for them. It soon became evident that more explicit national guidance was required. For this reason, the Executive Board, in 1914, authorized "the appointment of a Director of Education when finances permit."

In 1916, "finances permitted" the establishment of a Department of Education. The main purposes of the new department were "to give leadership in a series of conferences for Scoutmasters and other Scout officials throughout the country . . . to promote and develop training courses for leadership in Scouting . . . to develop correspondence courses for inspiration and instruction for Scout leaders."

The training of volunteer leaders was, at last, firmly established. It became increasingly important by West's insistence that "the three greatest needs" of the Boy Scouts of America were "1—Training. 2—More training. 3—Yet more training."

In 1928, the Volunteer Training Service (by which name the department for Scoutmastership training was now known) inaugurated a "Five-Year Progressive Training Program" leading up to a new training award, the "Scoutmaster's Key" (later changed to "Scouter's Key").

During the years that followed, the training program was

further modified—most recently in 1956 when a new plan went into effect, consisting of a short course covering the fundamentals of Scouting and more extensive courses on the operation and program of the Scout units.

In doing so much for the adult leader, the significant educational feature of the Boy Scout program of providing leadership opportunities to boys was not lost sight of.

The emphasis on the importance of the patrol leader has grown over the years, and his training has been extended. In addition to the training the boy leader gets through his own Scoutmaster and through the *Handbook for Patrol Leaders*, published in 1929, many local councils offer special "junior leaders' training" events. Here not only patrol leaders but other boy leaders in Scouting have a chance to increase their leadership abilities.

With the establishment of Cub Scouting in 1933, the training work of the National Council was further expanded. Handbooks for Cubmasters, Den Mothers, and den chiefs set the pattern for the work in packs and dens, but because of the special features of Cub Scouting a training method different from that used in Boy Scouting had to be developed. The fundamentals could be handled in the same fashion but the advanced work had to be done in some other way since Cub Scouting is a home-centered program and not a program of the outdoors. One of the most effective developments in Cub Scouting leadership training has therefore been the "pow wow" at which leaders of packs and dens from a whole district or council gather in an exciting, fun-filled session to share ideas and learn new methods.

In Exploring, the leadership training takes place at conferences of elected and commissioned Explorer leaders.

At the first annual meeting of the Boy Scouts of America in 1911, James E. West, reporting on the membership, stated that "there are 4,000 Scoutmasters connected with the organization—2,000 of whom have actually registered at Headquarters."

On its fiftieth anniversary, the Boy Scouts of America counts in its membership close to 600,000 dedicated adult leaders working directly with boys as Scoutmasters and assistant Scoutmasters, Cubmasters and assistant Cubmasters, Den Mothers, Explorer Advisors and associate Advisors. All of these are volunteers, giving their time and efforts willingly and unstintingly, guiding boys toward the Scouting goal of good citizenship.

Den Chief

TRAINING FOR CUB SCOUTING

Patrol Leader

CUB
SCOUT
UNIT

UNIT LEADER

CHAIRMAN

UNIT
COMMITTEEMEN

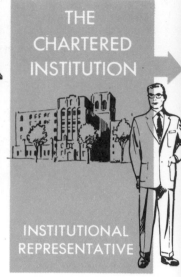

THE
CHARTERED
INSTITUTION

INSTITUTIONAL
REPRESENTATIVE

BOY
SCOUT
UNIT

UNIT LEADER

CHAIRMAN

UNIT
COMMITTEEMEN

THE
CHARTERED
INSTITUTION

INSTITUTIONAL
REPRESENTATIVE

EXPLORER
SCOUT
UNIT

UNIT LEADER

CHAIRMAN

UNIT
COMMITTEEMEN

THE
CHARTERED
INSTITUTION

INSTITUTIONAL
REPRESENTATIVE

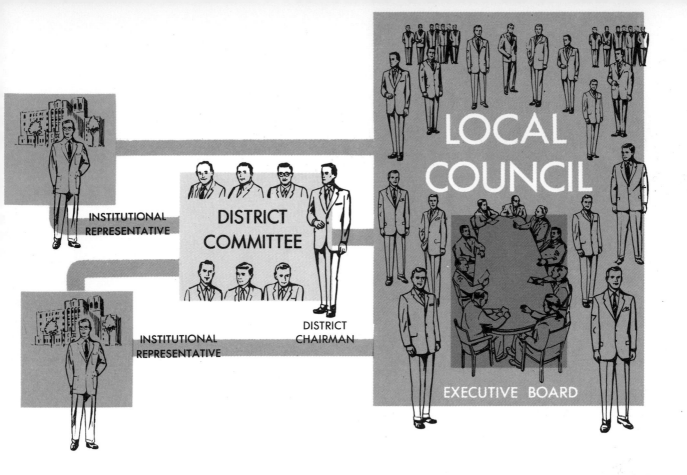

Local Organization

One of the big problems of early Scouting was the here-today-gone-tomorrow existence of numerous Scout troops. Many men rushed in willingly to give their services—but a number of them discovered that they were either not qualified or that Scouting took too much of their time. They dropped out—with the result that the troops disintegrated and the boys were robbed of the chance of being Scouts.

This problem was thoroughly discussed at a Scout commissioners' conference in November, 1912. Out of this conference came an idea which was promptly accepted in America: "Line up behind the Scoutmaster a small committee of men from the community who will support him and agree to find a successor for him if he should leave."

This idea was placed before the third annual meeting of the Boy Scouts of America on February 11, 1913, and received unanimous approval as a recommended procedure: " . . . in the interests of making the work of the troop permanent and securing necessary support, in many cases it will prove helpful to have a troop committee of three or five men interested in Scouting."

THE MEN BEHIND
THE MAN BEHIND
THE BOYS

Policy and permanency

Program and facilities

Outdoor program

Finances and property

But who was to get the idea "on the road"? In those early days, it was the Scoutmaster, as per instructions in the first *Handbook for Scoutmasters:*

"The applicant for the Scoutmaster's commission is required to organize a troop committee, consisting of three or five representative men of the community, preferably members of the organization with which the troop is connected, to supervise the work of the troop. This committee should endorse the application of the Scoutmaster and agree to co-operate with him in carrying out the Scout program should a commission be granted."

Scoutmasters already commissioned were not required to line up a committee. But they were strongly urged to give "careful consideration to the advantages of providing such a committee."

The troop committee idea caught on. When new troop registration blanks went into effect on October 1, 1913, space was provided for three men to agree "to co-operate with the applicant in carrying out the Scout program in accordance with the official handbooks, by encouraging the Scoutmaster and the boys in their work from time to time in such ways as may be feasible." The "troop committee or representative citizens" further agreed that: "If for any reason the Scoutmaster discontinues to serve we will notify the National Council immediately and endeavor to find a suitable successor and meanwhile assume control of the troop, including all troop property."

At its meeting in May, 1914, the Executive Board determined that "the provision for a troop committee, heretofore merely a recommendation, will be required hereafter of all new troops and with all reregistering troops after October 1."

The troop committee had become a permanent fixture of the organization of the Boy Scouts of America.

This committee of "three or more male citizens of the United States" quickly proved one of the most steadying influences in the life of a Scout troop. And it soon became the troop committee's task to secure a Scoutmaster, rather than the other way around.

The responsibilities of the troop committee have been expanded from time to time. Today they include the selection of a leader, advising him on questions of policy, helping him in the observance of the rules and regulations of the Boy Scouts of America, and encouraging him in carrying out the activities of Scouting, with special emphasis on assuring every

Boy Scout a year-round outdoor program. The troop committee is also responsible for providing meeting facilities, for the finances and property of the troop, for ensuring the troop's permanency, and for assuming active direction of it in case the leader is unable to serve, until his successor has been appointed and commissioned.

When Cub Scouting started in 1930, the committee principle was incorporated in its organization, and each pack was required to have a pack committee. Similarly, in Exploring, each unit has a post committee responsible for helping the Explorer advisor in his work and for ensuring the permanency of the unit.

Today there are over 620,000 adults in all parts of the United States serving on Boy Scout, Cub Scout, and Exploring unit committees.

THE EARLIEST INTENTION was that the men making up the troop committee should, preferably, be "members of the organization with which the troop is connected."

THE CHARTERED INSTITUTION

This was in keeping with the announcement in the 1911 *Handbook for Boys* that: "The aim of the Boy Scouts is to supplement the various existing educational agencies . . . It is not the aim to set up a new organization to parallel in its purposes others already established. The opportunity is afforded these organizations, however, to introduce into their programs unique features appealing to interests which are universal among boys."

Organizations around the country took the Boy Scouts at their word. They immediately started to look into the possibility of using the Scout program to further their own aims. They found it easy to do so. The ideals and purposes of the Boy Scout movement were so completely in harmony with the spirit and the goals of the organizations—churches, schools, civic clubs, and others—that it became a simple matter for them to build a partnership with the Boy Scouts of America.

The Church of Jesus Christ of Latter-day Saints—the "Mormon" Church—established a committee on Scouting in 1913 and was the first church to adopt, as a body, the program of the Boy Scouts of America and to integrate it closely to its own program for boys.

In 1916 the Federal Charter gave further impetus to this trend by flatly stating that Scouting was to be extended "through organization, and co-operation with other agencies." To further this desirable trend, the Protestant Committee on Scouting was formed in 1923, the Catholic Committee in 1924, and the Jewish Committee in 1926. Other denominations have similarly accepted Scouting in their work with boys.

In like manner, educational groups have taken up Scouting. Some of America's leading educators have wholeheartedly endorsed Scouting and use it in their schools. The P.T.A. is among the largest sponsors of Cub Scout packs, Boy Scout troops, and Explorer posts.

Service clubs—Lions, Rotary, Kiwanis, Exchange, and others; veterans' organizations—the American Legion, the Veterans of Foreign Wars, Amvets; the AFL-CIO; farm organizations—National Grange, American Farm Bureau, Farmer Co-operatives; civic groups—fire and police departments, chambers of commerce; youth-serving organizations—the YMCA, Boys' Clubs, 4H Clubs, FFA, and others—all have endorsed the Scouting program and co-operate locally in organizing Scout units within their groups.

The result of this extraordinary good will and confidence has been that, today, more than 82,000 local institutions receive charters from the Boy Scouts of America to maintain Scout units. They also join hands with each other in forming local councils which serve the units and extend Scouting to all boys of every creed and color.

ORGANIZATION OF THE LOCAL COUNCIL

DISTRICT CHAIRMEN

LOCAL COUNCIL

REPRESENTATIVE ON NATIONAL COUNCIL

WITH THE SUDDEN, overwhelming acceptance of the Scouting idea by the boys of the United Kingdom in 1908, Baden-Powell found himself in a dilemma. He expected that existing organizations would be able to take care of the boys. Instead, patrols and troops set out on their own. Some discriminating supervision in the appointment of Scoutmasters and in the bestowal of Scout badges was required if Scouting was to keep its good name.

Baden-Powell solved the problem by suggesting the establishment of "local committees" in every city "where gentlemen will be so good as to serve upon them." He further asked such committees on taking up their duties to "forward to my manager the name and address of the gentleman who will act as their secretary."

The founders of the Boy Scouts of America realized that American Scouting would most certainly encounter the same problem and determined to meet it squarely from the start.

At a meeting on June 21, 1910, Edgar M. Robinson proposed the establishment of a Committee on Organization to arrange for a permanent plan of local as well as national organization. The urgency of the matter was further emphasized at the October meeting of the Committee by the report of Managing

THE LOCAL COUNCIL

HEALTH AND SAFETY

ORGANIZATION AND EXTENSION

FINANCE

EXECUTIVE BOARD

ADVANCEMENT

CAMPING AND ACTIVITIES

LEADERSHIP TRAINING

THE COUNCIL
Includes all institutional representatives and a minority of members at large. Elects council officers:
   Council President
   Vice Presidents
   Council Commissioner
   Treasurer
   National Council Representatives
   Members of the Executive Board

THE EXECUTIVE BOARD
Includes:
   District Chairmen
   Council Officers
   Chairman of each council operating committee:
      Health and Safety
      Organization and Extension
      Finance
      Advancement
      Leadership Training
      Camping Activities

Secretary John L. Alexander: "The safety of the movement lies in its leadership, and I believe that the only way that this can be safeguarded is through the formation of local committees which will act upon these matters. To organize these committees properly it is necessary to have a decent field staff at work among the cities in our country."

By the end of 1910, two hundred of these local committees—now called local councils—had been established. It became one of James E. West's functions to strengthen them and to provide for their spread into every community where Scouting had been established.

While the first local councils were composed of "representative business men of all sects and creeds," by 1913 it was specified that any institution or organization forming a troop to carry out the Boy Scout program "should be invited to designate an adult representative other than the Scoutmaster to serve as a member of the local council." This was the emergence of the "institutional representative" whose functions were to become increasingly important as the years went by.

THE SCOUT COMMISSIONER

Another Scout official emerging from the earliest attempts at local organization was the Scout commissioner—a volunteer who would act as the local authority on Scoutcraft and could give considerable time to working directly with the troops of his community.

In practice it was soon found that while the Scout commissioner, as a kind of volunteer executive secretary, could give the necessary leadership in smaller communities, in larger cities the work was too much for a volunteer. To be successful, the local council needed full-time workers.

Out of this situation evolved two classes of local councils: the first class council which maintained an office with one or more employed officials giving all their time to the promotion of Scouting, and the second class council organized in communities where the work was not sufficiently developed to permit the employment of a "Scout executive."

These two methods of local organization worked side by side for a number of years across America, affording a laboratory test as to which was the more effective.

By the close of the first decade, the advantages of the first class council had been so clearly demonstrated that the time was considered ripe to bring the entire country under this plan. The responsibility for this project was turned over to Dr. George J. Fisher, who, in 1919, had become Deputy Chief Scout Executive. The task was completed in 1931.

Today, 532 chartered local councils cover every part of the United States. These councils range in size from a single community to an entire state. For efficiency in operation, they divide their territories into districts. By this decentralized organization, 2,848 districts form the basic administrative organization through which councils serve existing Cub Scout packs, Boy Scout troops, and Explorer posts and work to bring Scouting to all boys.

The council body is made up of representatives from each group sponsoring a Scouting unit, plus members at large. This body elects an executive board which then assumes the responsibility for Scouting within the council area. The Scout executive and his staff work largely through volunteers—the council and district committees, each responsible for a phase of the operation; and the commissioner staff, which gives direct assistance to the units and their leaders.

The committees are responsible for the organization of new units and the general extension of Scouting, the training of volunteer leaders, the development of camps, the planning of activities, the financing of the council, and the Scouts' advancement, health, and safety.

Altogether, more than eighty thousand volunteer council Scouters—district and neighborhood commissioners, and members of district and council committees—work on the local level to give help and support to the leaders who work directly with the boys.

THE SCOUT EXECUTIVE

Ellsworth H. Augustus

National Organization

HONORARY OFFICERS

DWIGHT D. EISENHOWER
Honorary President
HERBERT HOOVER
Honorary Vice President
HARRY S. TRUMAN
Honorary Vice President

AMORY HOUGHTON
Honorary Vice President
JOHN M. SCHIFF
Honorary Vice President
KENNETH K. BECHTEL
Honorary Vice President

NATIONAL OFFICERS

ELLSWORTH H. AUGUSTUS
President *
WILLIAM D. CAMPBELL
Vice President
NORTON CLAPP
Vice President
WM. HARRISON FETRIDGE
Vice President
WHEELER McMILLEN
Vice President
THOMAS J. WATSON, JR.
Vice President

GEORGE J. FISHER
National Scout Commissioner
ELBERT K. FRETWELL
Chief Scout
WILLIAM D. CAMPBELL
International Commissioner
GERALD F. BEAL
Treasurer
ARTHUR A. SCHUCK
Chief Scout Executive

* *For information about past presidents
of the National Council, see pages 160–161.*

ADVISORY COUNCIL

CHARLES E. COTTING
J. M. T. FINNEY, JR.
PHILIP L. REED
EDWARD V. RICKENBACKER
R. DOUGLAS STUART

EXECUTIVE BOARD

THE NATIONAL COUNCIL is responsible for the functioning of the Boy Scouts of America. This body of over five thousand people is made up of representatives of each local council, supplemented by honorary members and members at large— the latter group chosen mostly from among regional and national committees. It governs the movement through an Executive Board of not more than fifty-one members plus regional members and life members, elected at its annual meetings. This board, in turn, elects the Chief Scout Executive and expects him, as the executive officer of the Boy Scouts of America, to be responsible for the actual operation of the movement.

ORGANIZATION OF THE NATIONAL STAFF

ASST'S. TO CHIEF SCOUT EXEC.

SPECIAL ASSIGNMENTS

FULFILLMENT

I. B. M.

OFFICE SERV.

PHILLIPS PROPERTIES

ASSISTANT CHIEF SCOUT EXECUTIVE

J

RELATIONSHIP DIV.

I

PERSONNEL DIV.

G

PROGRAM

H

PUBLIC RELATIONS

F

EDUCATIONAL DIV.

E

RESEARCH SERV.

B

FIELD

A

FINANCE SERVICE

BE PREPARED

BOY SCOUTS OF AMERICA

CHIEF SCOUT EXECUTIVE

DEPUTY CHIEF SCOUT EXECUTIVE

COMPTROLLER

D

BOYS' LIFE

SUPPLY DIVISION

A. FINANCE SERVICE assists local councils in matters pertaining to financial support.

B. FIELD OPERATIONS directs the work of the twelve regional offices.

C. SUPPLY SERVICE DIVISION directs manufacture, purchase, distribution, and sale of uniforms, equipment, insignia, and books.

D. BOYS' LIFE supervises all phases in creation of the official Boy Scout magazine.

E. RESEARCH SERVICE directs all research projects and experiments.

F. EDUCATIONAL DIVISION
> *Editorial Service*—creates Scouting literature and manages periodicals for leaders.
> *Printing and Production Service*—buys paper and contracts for printing.
> *Visual Education Service*—produces training film strips and movies.
> *Volunteer Training Service*—develops training experiences for volunteer leaders. Supervises volunteer training at Philmont and Schiff Scout Reservation.

G. PROGRAM DIVISION deals directly with all Scouting activities. The basic work of the Cub Scouting, Boy Scouting, and Exploring Services is supplemented by—
> *Camping Service*—promotes outdoor programs.
> *Engineering Service*—helps develop camp property and other physical facilities.
> *Health and Safety Service*—sets standards and develops program in these fields.
> *Activities and Special Events Service*—develops program ideas for large-scale events.
> *Program Resources Service*—assists in developing new program activities and literature.

H. PUBLIC RELATIONS SERVICE works to develop public knowledge and correct understanding of the Boy Scouts of America.

I. PERSONNEL DIVISION selects and trains professional leaders; manages Schiff Reservation. Deals with volunteers and clerical personnel. Supervises Statistical Service.

J. RELATIONSHIP DIVISION deals with institutions and organizations that use Scout program in their work with boys. Includes Protestant, Catholic, "Mormon," and Jewish Services, Civic Service, School Service, Interracial, Rural, and International Services.

NATIONAL STAFF

Among his many duties, the Chief Scout Executive has the responsibility of appointing the members of the national staff and directing their work. This task was comparatively easy while the movement was young but has grown increasingly complex during the years.

James E. West, on taking office in January of 1911, immediately set up several "departments" and "bureaus" to handle various aspects of the work. Under the 1917 constitution, the national staff was reorganized into six departments: Field, Educational, Library, Camping, Publication, and Supply.

During the following years, more departments were added: Registration, Relationships, Professional Training, Rural Scouting, Interracial Scouting, and others—all of them answerable directly to the Chief Scout Executive.

The burden of carrying these responsibilities finally caused James E. West to ask the Executive Board to authorize a thorough study by outside specialists of the operation of the national organization. The results of this investigation was the recommendation that the nearly two dozen "departments" be grouped into four "divisions," each with an executive director.

This "divisional plan" was adopted by the Executive Board.

On January 1, 1931, the former "departments" became "services" in the new "divisions."

In 1957 the organization of the national staff was further decentralized through the creation of two positions of Assistant Chief Scout Executive working directly under the Chief Scout Executive. These two men share with the Deputy Chief Scout Executive and with two Assistants to the Chief Scout Executive, the supervision of all national staff functions.

The Deputy Chief Scout Executive, in addition to his other responsibilities, gives direct leadership to Field Operations, which directs the work of twelve regional offices; and to the Supply Service Division, which is responsible for the manufacture, purchase, distribution and sale of uniforms and equipment, insignia and books of the Boy Scouts of America. He also supervises the Finance Service, which assists councils in all matters pertaining to adequate financial support; as well as the work of the BOYS' LIFE magazine staff.

One Assistant Chief Scout Executive, in addition to other responsibilities, has supervision over the Program Division, the Education Division and the Research Service.

The Program Division deals most directly with the activities of Scouting as they affect the boy. The three basic services are Cub Scouting, Boy Scouting, and Exploring. Supplementing these are: the Camping Service, responsible for the promotion of an adventurous all-year outdoor program; the Engineering Service, which helps councils develop camp property and other physical facilities; the Health and Safety Service, which sets standards in these important fields; and the Activities and Special Events Service, which develops program ideas in large scale Scouting events. The Program Resources Service assists in the development of new program activities.

The Education Division, through its Editorial Service, is charged with the creation of Scouting literature and the management of periodicals for leaders in all phases of the program. The purchase of paper and contracting for printing is the responsibility of the Printing and Production Service. The Visual Education Service prepares training helps in the form of film strips and movies, and the Volunteer Training Service develops training experiences for all categories of Scout volunteers including the supervision of the volunteer training centers at Philmont and Schiff Scout Reservation.

The Research Service gives direction to all research projects and experiments conducted by the national organization.

The other Assistant Chief Scout Executive, in addition to special duties, supervises the work of the Personnel Division, the Relationships Division, and the Public Relations Service.

The Personnel Division is responsible for the selection and training of professional leaders and the management of the Schiff Scout Reservation. It also deals with the procurement, certification, and recognition of volunteers and with the securing and welfare of clerical personnel. The Statistical Service is one of the functions of the Personnel Division.

In the Relationships Division are gathered the services dealing with institutions and organizations that use the Scout program in their work with boys: the Catholic, Jewish, "Mormon," Protestant, School, and Civic Relationships Service. This division also includes services working with special groups: Interracial, Rural and International.

The Public Relations Service is responsible for the development of public knowledge and correct understanding of the purposes and activities of the Boy Scouts of America.

One Assistant to the Chief Scout Executive is directly responsible for the national office services, IBM, Subscription Fulfillment, and Central Typing Service. The other Assistant to the Chief Scout Executive supervises the operation of Phillips Properties, including Philmont and the Philtower office building in Tulsa, Oklahoma.

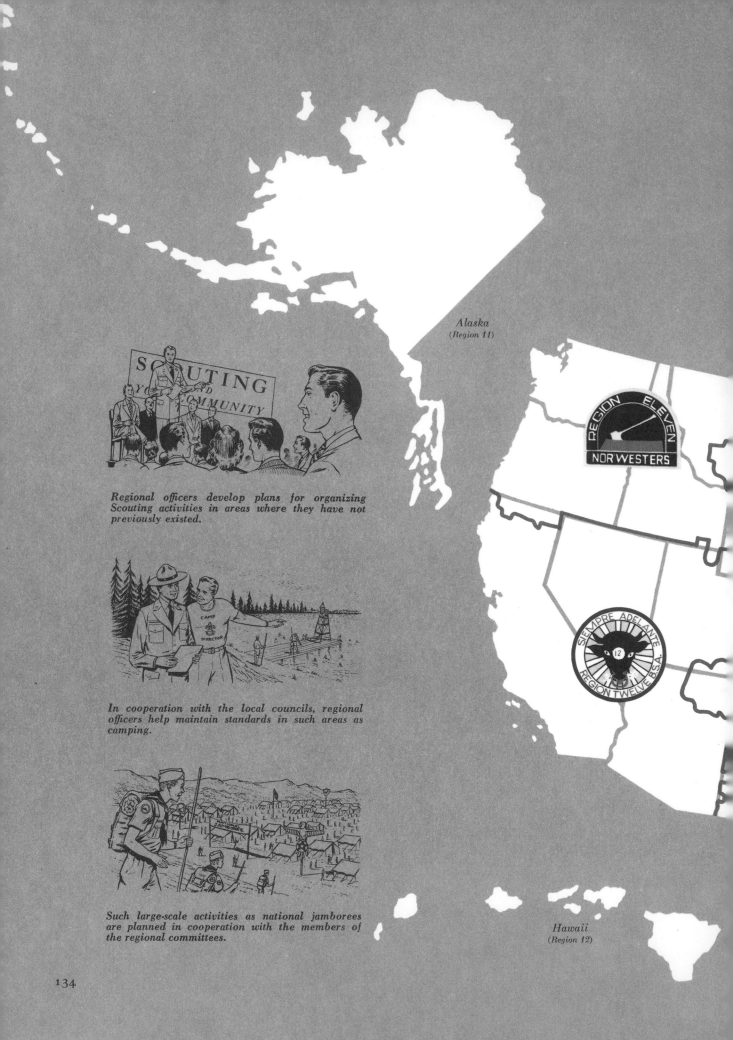

Regional officers develop plans for organizing Scouting activities in areas where they have not previously existed.

In cooperation with the local councils, regional officers help maintain standards in such areas as camping.

Such large-scale activities as national jamborees are planned in cooperation with the members of the regional committees.

Alaska
(Region 11)

Hawaii
(Region 12)

In the early development of the United States into local councils, special commissioners working out of the National Council did much of the spade work. In 1913, three traveling national field commissioners covered the East, the Middle West, and the Pacific Coast. In 1918, six districts were formed and manned with traveling commissioners.

In 1919, the country was divided into 12 regions, following closely the geographical lines of the Federal Reserve System. Each region has an office and is assigned members of the national staff who are supported in their direct help to local councils by a volunteer regional committee.

Through the years, each region has developed its own spirit and personality and each strives to excel in the job that is done.

TWELVE REGIONS

Puerto Rico
(Region 2)

Canal Zone
(Region 6)

Scouting Marches On

The "little black book"

NATIONAL OFFICE

IN A SAFE in the national office of the Boy Scouts of America, among other historical documents, lies a little black book. Open it and skim its pages. In neat lines, page after page, are written down the locations of early troops and the names of their Scoutmasters. A little black book was all that was needed in those first days of 1910 and 1911 to keep track of the growth of the infant movement.

Today the registration service of the national office has on file the names of one and a third million adults and close to four million boys—all active members of the Boy Scouts of America.

From yesterday's little black book to today's files—there, in tangible form, is one of the proofs of the tremendous vitality of the Scouting "baby."

Everything else in the Boy Scouts of America testifies to the same amazing growth.

Take the national office itself, for instance.

The first office soon outgrew its temporary quarters in the Boys' Work department of the 28th Street Y.M.C.A. building in New York City, where it was located during its "teething" days in 1910. On January 2, 1911, the new movement opened its own office in the Fifth Avenue Building, 200 Fifth Avenue, with a staff of seven people. Within a few years, this office had spread to two floors of the large building.

By 1927, the space had become too cramped for the work and the personnel. The office moved—this time to 2 Park Avenue, New York. Here again, space was soon at a premium. To make room for expansion, the Supply Service was moved to another building and the main office took over the space that was vacated.

In the early 1950's the national office was once more faced with lack of space—and also with expiring long-term leases and increased rentals. A permanent solution was required.

The Executive Board appointed a committee to look into the situation. After an exhaustive study, the committee recommended the erection of a national office building suited to the current and the future needs of the movement.

After further study to determine a proper location, one hundred acres were purchased a couple of miles south of New Brunswick, New Jersey. Here a two-story office building and a one-story warehouse were constructed. On October 1, 1954, the national office moved into its own quarters.

The new office proved a tremendous boon to efficiency. It also made still greater service possible to local councils and units across the country.

Every day, the telephone switchboard of the national office handles 1,500 calls, the warehouse ships approximately 2,000 orders, the registration service types out 750 unit charters and 30,000 individual membership certificates. Every month, the mailing department processes half a million pieces of mail, the subscription fulfillment service prepares three million labels for mailing SCOUTING magazine and BOYS' LIFE.

In addition to providing working facilities for more than seven hundred people, the national office has become a pilgrimage site for thousands of Scout-interested visitors traveling through New Jersey on Routes 1 and 130.

These visits will increase immeasurably when the historical museum of the Boy Scouts of America opens its doors—the gift of Mr. Gale F. Johnston, Executive Board member, in memory of his wife. The exhibits of this museum will tell the story of the birth of the Scout movement and its growth—not only in America but all around the globe.

Entrance to National office with Boy Scout statue by R. Tait McKenzie

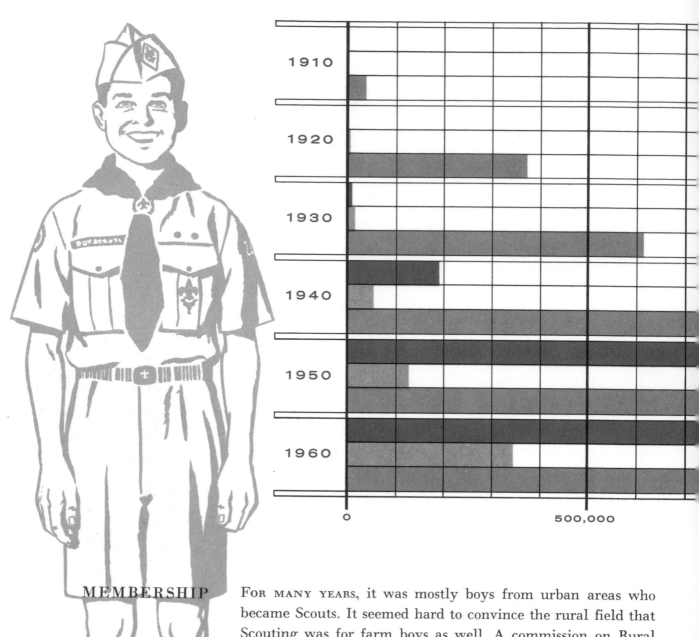

1910

1920

1930

1940

1950

1960

0   500,000

MEMBERSHIP

FOR MANY YEARS, it was mostly boys from urban areas who became Scouts. It seemed hard to convince the rural field that Scouting was for farm boys as well. A commission on Rural Scouting, established in 1924, studied the problem and, with the cooperation of the Agriculture Extension Service and farm organizations and other rural agencies, developed a complete report on rural Scout needs. The result was the establishment of a Rural Scouting Service in 1926, with the subsequent spectacular growth of Scout membership in rural areas, passing the million mark in 1957.

Another field in which boys and their parents seemed to "hold back" was among minority groups. From the very start, the movement had emphasized that Scouting was for all boys of all races and creeds—yet few Negro boys, Indian boys, or Latin-American boys had joined. If the boys didn't come to Scouting, Scouting would have to go to them.

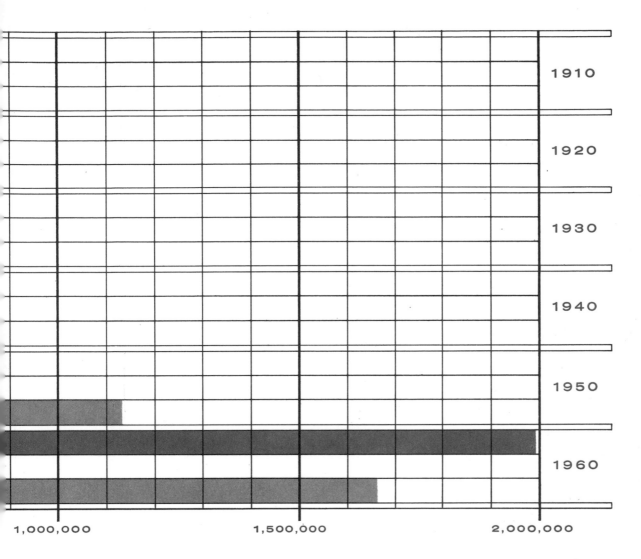

	1,000,000		1,500,000		2,000,000

Cub Scout

Explorer

Boy Scout

The first great step in this direction was the proposal by a Scouters' conference in 1924 that a concerted effort be made to extend Scouting to Negro boys in the South. Within two years, the national office could report 248 troops with close to five thousand Negro Scouts under Negro leadership. To give further impetus to this development, an Interracial Service was created in 1927.

The work in the Indian field received a great boost in 1929 when the Secretary of the Interior requested national cooperation in bringing Scouting to boys on Indian reservations. Tribal councils and American Indian organizations took up the cause and have joined forces in extending Scouting.

In the ever-growing membership are also included a large and increasing number of handicapped Scouts. This again dramatizes the fact that Scouting is for all boys—not just for the fit, but also for the handicapped.

SCOUT CAMPING

"By the term 'scouting,'" wrote Baden-Powell, "is meant the work and attributes of backwoodsmen, explorers, hunters, seamen, airmen, pioneers, and frontiersmen."

The very word "Scout" opened up to the boys of the world the picture of the woods, rivers, lakes, and mountains that were to be their playground where they were to have fun.

It was this promise of life in the outdoors that caused American boys to flock into Scouting, and set out for the wide open spaces to build fires, broil—or burn, as the case might be— the meat brought from the family pantry, and return home, tired and dirty, from a great and happy experience.

To boys, outdoor life was fun, romance, adventure. To their leaders it was that, too—and much more: They saw in hiking and camping the means toward character development, citizenship training, and physical fitness.

The incorporators of the Boy Scouts of America were fully aware of the educational values of the outdoor activities of Scouting. When appearing before the Committee on Education of the House of Representatives in March, 1910, in an early effort to secure Federal incorporation of the new movement, they stated: "If boys are to grow into sturdy, self-reliant, productive citizens they must have much outdoor life and get the training in personal initiative and resourcefulness, keenness of perception and alertness in action, courage, cheerful obedience, ability to command, self-control, ability to do teamwork and the other manly qualities that can be developed in healthy outdoor sport."

Permanent camp and training center

Weekend camp

140

Until the advent of Scouting, relatively few people had taken camping seriously. Certain youth groups had developed "organized camps," as had a number of individual educators and outdoor enthusiasts. But to the general public, camping was a form of recreation for the few who could afford it—a pleasant recreation with beneficial aspects, but certainly with no appeal to the masses.

Scouting profoundly changed this attitude. It put the spotlight on camping as a character-influencing factor, as an education for living, and therefore as an ally in the work of the home, the school, and the church. It built up the tradition that boys can be depended on to take care of themselves on the trail and in camp.

By the summer of Scouting's first year, forests and parks resounded with the pounding of tent stakes and the merry laughter of happy boys. Scoutmasters to whom camping was a new experience carried through to the best of their abilities on camp sites lent to their troops by obliging farmers.

During the following years, national "minimum standards" for Boy Scout camps were developed and adopted, and Scout camping improved immeasurably. During the same period, as local councils became more and more firmly established, people realized that Scouting had come to stay. With this realization came the awareness that while Scout membership was growing, the wilderness areas of America were dwindling. Something had to be done, if the Scouts of the future were to have the outdoor life to which they were entitled.

Wilderness camp

PHILMONT SCOUT RANCH
THE WORLD'S BIGGEST BOYS' CAMP—127,000 ACRES OF THE OLD
MAXWELL LAND GRANT IN N.E. NEW MEXICO AND DEDICATED TO SCOUT-
ING BY MR. WAITE PHILLIPS IN 1938. TIME AT PHILMONT IS FOR MOUNTAIN-SIZED
ADVENTURE, MOVEMENT THROUGH PRIMITIVE BACK-COUNTRY BEAUTY, THRILL-PACKED
DAYS IN THE LAND OF THE MOUNTAIN MEN OF KIT CARSON'S DAYS. TROUT
FISHING, MOUNTAIN CLIMBING, TRAIL RIDING, CAMPING, PANNING FOR GOLD IN A RUG-
GED TRADITION-FILLED LAND LEAVES SCOUTS WITH UNFORGETTABLE MEMORIES SUCH
AS THESE EXPLORERS GATHER ON THE TRAIL TO THE FABLED "TOOTH OF TIME".

Norman Rockwell

The outcome was the acquisition by local councils of numerous permanent campsites. Many of these were given to the Boy Scouts by local service clubs, other groups of citizens, and individual donors. A number were purchased by special funds raised by the councils.

Today, the number of permanent campsites owned by the local councils of the Boy Scouts of America has grown to 829. These campsites cover approximately 554,800 acres, which Scouts can truly call their own. No other organized group in America has a larger number of campers.

LOCAL
CAMPING
AREAS

In addition to these campsites, the National Council owns two important training and camping reservations that benefit Scouts and Explorers throughout the country.

The first of these—the Mortimer L. Schiff Scout Reservation at Mendham, New Jersey—was presented to the Boy Scouts in 1933 by Mrs. Jacob Schiff in memory of her son, National President of the Boy Scouts of America at the time of his death in 1931. Part of the Reservation's 480 acres of rolling, wooded hills are set aside for the training of camp directors and junior leaders. But the Reservation's main functions are to serve as a training center for professional Scouters and for short conferences for volunteer leaders.

NATIONAL
RESERVATIONS

The second national reservation is the Philmont Scout Ranch of more than 127,000 acres in the Rocky Mountains near Cimarron, New Mexico. This ranch and mountain property was given to the Boy Scouts of America by Mr. Waite Phillips, a Tulsa, Oklahoma, oil executive, to provide a large, exciting area where Explorers and older Scouts from every part of the United States could enjoy the thrill of real Western camping. Philmont is rich in the history of the Southwestern Indian, hard-riding conquistadores, early American trappers and frontiersmen. Its prairies, foothills, and canyons abound with wildlife—deer, elk, coyote, antelope, mountain lion, buffalo, and bear. Its streams teem with trout. On foot or on horseback, Explorer campers—as many as 10,000 a year— travel into the mountain fastnesses of Philmont for one of the most exciting adventures of their Scouting lives.

At the same time, adult leadership training opportunities are provided at the Philmont Volunteer Training Center, where, each week during the summer, 400 Scouting families gather for Scouting courses, combined with fun and recreation.

Scout camping has come of age as a challenging and resourceful character building aspect of the Scouting program. Camping is, as it has always been, the heartbeat of Scouting.

Scouting campsites are located all over the United States.

★ *Philmont Scout Ranch*
● *Schiff Scout Reservation*

PHILMONT SCOUT RANCH *by Norman Rockwell*

HANDBOOKS

THE MEMBERS of the Boy Scouts of America are voracious readers—at least of their own handbooks. More than three million manuals for the different phases of Scouting come off the printing presses every year.

Cub Scouts of varying age levels pore over their three handbooks—the *Wolf Cub*, the *Bear Cub*, and the *Lion Cub Book*. Cubmasters, Den Mothers, and den chiefs all have their own handbooks. In Boy Scouting, the *Boy Scout Handbook* and the *Scout Field Book* are popular among the boys. Patrol leaders and Scoutmasters seek help in their respective handbooks. In Exploring, Explorers and their Advisors share the same book.

Of all these books, one—the *Boy Scout Handbook*—has achieved special fame. Next to the Holy Bible it is the largest American best seller of all time. In its various editions it has reached a distribution of close to seventeen million copies—and the sales are steadily increasing.

In addition to being the largest seller of all Scout books, it also has the most interesting story behind it.

When the Boy Scout movement reached the United States in 1910, Baden-Powell's *Scouting for Boys* was imported with it. But this was a British book, telling British boys of their duties to Britain, using British heroes to inspire them.

The sudden, tremendous interest in the Boy Scouts in the United States called for the speedy production of an American book on Scouting, with special appeal to American boys.

The task of getting out such a book was thrown into the lap

of Ernest Thompson Seton. He solved it in short order by combining about fifty pages on Scouting from Baden-Powell's book with approximately one hundred pages on American woodcraft and Indian lore taken from his own writings. The resulting volume appeared in July, 1910, under the title of *Boy Scouts of America—Official Handbook*.

Within a year, close to seventy thousand copies of this first attempt at an American handbook were sold—an extraordinary number for a boys' book in those days.

The work on the preparation of a more adequate handbook was immediately begun.

The big question was, "What kind of book will best serve the American boy?" After much deliberation, the Editorial Board and the newly appointed Chief Scout Executive James E. West decided that the book was to be a compendium of separate chapters on the different aspects of Scouting. Leading specialists in the various fields—naturalists and explorers, doctors, and experts on citizenship—were called upon to prepare sections of the book. When finally the committees that had been established to standardize the Scout Oath and Law, requirements and badges, had completed their work and had presented their findings, the book was ready to go to press.

1910

1911

1914

1927

1940

1947

146

1950

But in spite of the urgent need, West held back. He felt that it would be a mistake for the Boy Scouts of America to attempt to set a pattern of living and learning for the boyhood of America without sharing the responsibility with others.

The result was that the publication of the *Handbook for Boys* became a most unusual adventure in book publishing.

West asked the publishers—Doubleday, Page & Company—to furnish him with 4,500 proof copies to be sent to educators, superintendents of schools, boys' work directors, and boys' club secretaries all over the country, as well as to all Scout commissioners and Scoutmasters registered at the time. He wanted their reactions to this new book.

The publishers insisted that this was something that had never been done before. They finally agreed to make the copies available—provided West would arrange to have the sheets collated and would handle the distribution. West organized a working crew, borrowed the key to the publishing plant so that he and his crew could work at night, and transferred his office to Garden City, Long Island, where the plant was located.

Eleven days from the completion of the manuscript, the 4,500 copies of the proof edition were in the mails.

West allotted the readers thirty days to send back their suggestions and corrections. These were all tabulated and carefully considered, and many of them were incorporated.

At last the book was ready to go to press—probably the only book in history that has had the services of more than four thousand editors!

On August 31st, 1911, the first edition of 40,000 copies hit the book stores and was soon exhausted. During the first year, 160,000 were in print—with the Gordon Grant figure of a hat-waving Boy Scout on the cover.

A few years later, all chapters were thoroughly reviewed and some of them replaced. On the cover now appeared the famous J. C. Leyendecker painting of a buddy team of signaling Boy Scouts. With minor changes, this third edition remained the familiar *Handbook for Boys* for twenty-five printings of 100,000 copies each.

In November, 1927, a more modern version of the *Handbook* made its appearance. Again specialists had been called upon to present their subjects. Artists who were experts on nature and on Scoutcraft had prepared the illustrations. A special feature of this edition was the Norman Rockwell cover depicting the ideal Boy Scout, surrounded by American heroes.

When the Scout requirements were materially changed in 1947, a thorough remaking of the *Handbook* became necessary. This fifth edition was developed using new material especially prepared by experts in the fields of nature, Scoutcraft, campcraft, and citizenship.

With the approach of the Golden Jubilee of the Boy Scouts of America, the decision to publish a brand-new kind of handbook was made. This was to be a book illustrated completely in color and based squarely on the requirements leading the boy from Tenderfoot through Second Class, First Class, Star, Life, and Eagle to full-fledged citizenship—yet retaining the excitement of the outdoors, of hiking and camping and all the other activities that have caused millions upon millions of boys to become Scouts.

This new *Boy Scout Handbook*—the sixth in the series—with a cover figure painted especially for it by Norman Rockwell, makes its public appearance to coincide with the Fiftieth Anniversary of the Boy Scouts of America, in a first printing of 1,050,000 copies.

And more than ever before, this new edition of the *Boy Scout Handbook* will provide the perfect answer to the perennial question:

"If you were stranded on a desert island, which single book would you take with you . . . ?"

THE NEW HANDBOOK

Boy Scout Handbook 1960
Cover figure by Norman Rockwell

Norman Rockwell, beloved American artist

BOYS' LIFE 1912

BOYS' LIFE

FROM THE VERY BEGINNING, the Boy Scouts of America felt the need of being able to reach the individual boy directly for the purpose of helping him in his Scouting. The Executive Board also decided that one of the functions of the Boy Scout movement should be to provide the American boy with good reading.

In 1912, the Board formed a committee to look into the matter of a magazine for boys. The attention of this committee soon focused on Providence, Rhode Island.

Here, an eighteen-year old youth, Joseph Lane, had started a boys' magazine which he, in perfect good faith, called "the semi-official publication of the Boy Scouts of America, and the official organ of the Rhode Island Boy Scouts." He had hit on the ideal title for a boys' magazine: BOYS' LIFE.

After a number of conferences, Lane and his associates agreed to sell their magazine to the Boy Scouts of America for a sum equivalent to one dollar for each subscription actually on their books. The number was determined at 6,100—and the purchase price consequently at $6,100.

With the July 1912 issue of BOYS' LIFE, the Boy Scouts of America entered the magazine publishing business.

Early in 1913, a young man in his teens stepped into the office of BOYS' LIFE with samples of his art work. He was

immediately put to work painting a monthly cover and illustrating two to four stories for each issue. For this, the young artist was to receive the princely sum of $75 a month. Today this stripling artist ranks in a class by himself among American illustrators. His name? Norman Rockwell.

The Executive Board, in approving the purchase of the magazine, had stipulated that it must pay for itself. It was therefore with great satisfaction that Frank Presbrey, chairman of the BOYS' LIFE committee, could report, at the conclusion of the magazine's first year as Boy Scout property, a surplus of—$1.76.

The quality of BOYS' LIFE—its stories and articles, Scoutcraft and hobby features, color pages and illustrations—has steadily improved over the years.

The increasing appeal of this magazine "for all boys" to America's young readers is best shown by its amazing growth. Within seven years of its purchase by the Boy Scouts of America, the circulation had increased from 6,100 to 100,000. It reached one million in 1954.

BOYS' LIFE enters the Boy Scouts' golden jubilee with a circulation of two million copies a month. It ranks today not only as the largest youth magazine in the country but also as No. 14 in subscriptions among all American magazines.

THE GOOD TURN IDEA

THE GOOD TURN idea has been one of the prime concepts of Scouting from the beginning.

On becoming a Boy Scout the boy promises to "Help other people at all times." The Scout slogan reminds him to "Do a Good Turn daily." One of the points of the Scout Law specifies that "A Scout is helpful. . . . He must do at least one Good Turn to somebody every day."

The Boy Scout *Handbook* spells out what is meant by a Good Turn: "A Good Turn is an *extra* act of kindness—not just something you do because it is good manners. To answer the inquiry of someone on the street about an address is not a Good Turn—that is common courtesy. But to go out of your way to take the traveler to his destination—that's a Good Turn."

The Good Turn habit serves to help a boy become conscious of the people around him and to notice their needs. It influences his thinking and his actions as he gropes his way to manhood.

Mostly, a Good Turn is a small, thoughtful thing: helping a child across a street, picking a broken bottle off the highway, telephoning the power company to report a live wire, assisting someone in changing a tire. Such Good Turns are done and forgotten—even by the Scouts who do them.

Occasionally, a Good Turn becomes a matter of life or death.

A Scout drags a person out of a burning building, or pulls a drowning man out of the sea, or climbs into a well and brings up an unconscious child. In many cases of this nature the rescue involves quick thinking but little risk of life, in some the rescuer may be in deadly peril.

The records of the National Court of Honor contain the accounts of the deeds of these Scouts, who "forgetful of self, acted with courage and cool-headed resolve when the emergency struck." During the fifty years of the existence of the Boy Scouts of America, 1,313 Honor Medals have been awarded to Scouts, Explorers and Scouters for performing heroic life-saving action at the risk of their own lives.

LOCAL SERVICE

In addition to individual Good Turns, others are done on a patrol, unit or council basis. Some of these are deliberately planned as service to the community, others result from sudden emergencies.

In practically every great local calamity, Scouts are among the first relief forces on the scene. The Ohio floods of 1913 furnished the earliest important instance of this. The Massachusetts Scouts who were within call at the time of the Salem

Medal of Merit

A SCOUT IS HELPFUL *by Norman Rockwell*

Boy Scout service in the First World War

Boy Scout service in the Second World War

Peacetime Boy Scout service

fire in 1914 did excellent service. The munitions explosion which practically wrecked the town of South Amboy, New Jersey, in October, 1916, gave the Scouts of that community an opportunity to prove their worth. Hurricane-ravished areas —Florida in 1926, for instance, and New England in 1938— saw Scouts turn out in force to render aid. The same has happened almost yearly in flood-stricken regions—in Indiana, Arkansas, Mississippi, Ohio, Connecticut, and Pennsylvania, among others—where Scouts with boating and lifesaving skills have been of particular help.

The Good Turns undertaken on a national scale by the Boy Scouts of America have grown in scope and size over the years.

The first national Good Turn was performed in 1912 when the Boy Scouts helped promote a "Safe and Sane Fourth of July." The following year, Scouts did outstanding service to the Veterans of the Confederate and Northern Armies coming to Pennsylvania from the four corners of America for the 50th Anniversary of the Battle of Gettysburg.

The first World War revealed the tremendous potential power of a third of a million boys organized for service. The Scouts threw themselves whole-heartedly into helping their country. They sold more than $400,000,000 of Liberty Loan Bonds and $43,000,000 worth of War Savings Stamps. They located twenty thousand board feet of black walnut for gun stocks and airplane propellers. They collected over one hundred carloads of fruit pits for gas masks, cultivated twelve thousand war gardens, distributed thirty million pieces of Government literature, rendered invaluable service for the Red Cross and other national organizations.

Similar Good Turns on a national scale were performed by the Boy Scouts of America during the second World War. The Scouts collected aluminum and scrap iron, wastepaper and rubber, served with the Office of Civilian Defense, distributed Government posters and pamphlets as official dispatch bearers, raised food in "victory gardens."

The peacetime service record of the Boy Scouts of America has equalled the war record. It has involved "Get-Out-the-Vote" campaigns in presidential election years, national safety and conservation Good Turns, and many other kinds of service to the nation.

The Good Turn spirit and the capacity for service are stronger today than ever before as the steadily growing Scout movement in the United States enters upon its second half century.

NATIONAL SERVICE

Washington, D. C. 1937

Valley Forge

1950

1957

Southern California 1953

Colorado Springs 1960

WHEN SCOUTING in America approached its silver jubilee, plans were set in motion for some kind of spectacular celebration. The suggestion immediately presented itself: "The Boy Scouts of America was founded in Washington, D.C., in 1910. What could be more spectacular than to return to the nation's capital to celebrate the birthday with a tremendous gathering of Scouts from all over the country?" In other words, "Let's have a national jamboree!"

By the beginning of August, 1935, more than twenty thousand Scouts and leaders from every state in the Union and from several foreign countries had signed up and had started to converge on Washington from all the points of the compass.

Then lightning struck!

A serious epidemic of infantile paralysis had arisen in the vicinity of Washington. On August 8, the United States Public Health Service recommended that it would be too hazardous to hold the jamboree. President Franklin D. Roosevelt, as Honorary President of the Boy Scouts of America, went on the air to tell of the sad news: The jamboree had been cancelled!

Within two months, the Executive Board decided to go ahead with the plans for another jamboree two years hence.

On June 30, 1937, thirty-four thousand Scouts and leaders gathered in Washington. They pitched their tents below the Washington Monument, beside the Lincoln Memorial, in Potomac Park, and on Columbia Island.

This First National Jamboree was a memorable event with thousands of Scout actors performing in great arena shows . . . sightseeing hikes around Washington and boat excursions to Mount Vernon . . . large campfires and small and a review by the President of the United States of his fellow-Scouts lined up along Pennsylvania Avenue.

After the jamboree, Scouts and leaders alike agreed, "Let's have another before too long." But a war intervened, and it was not until 1950 that the Boy Scouts of America again invited its members to the Second National Jamboree at Valley Forge, Pennsylvania.

This time, forty-seven thousand Scouts and Explorers made camp on ground where Washington had trod, where his army had spent a desperate winter. The spirit of Washington was present at the big opening ceremony where the Valley Forge story was unfolded, and at the campfires that flared over the hillsides. One night, the nation's Scouts were joined by their country's chief executive, President Harry S. Truman. And another night the man who was destined to become the next

President of the United States, General Dwight D. Eisenhower, mingled with the campers.

For the Third National Jamboree in 1953, the Scouts went west and erected their tent city on the Irvine Ranch in Southern California, with a view of the vast Pacific from every campsite. The arrival of the contingents by trains and by buses, forty-five thousand strong, was the largest peacetime movement the country had ever witnessed. The days were full of fellowship and sunshine, the evenings of excitement, with Hollywood bringing in its stars to entertain the Scouts.

Four years later, fifty-two thousand boys again descended on Valley Forge for the Fourth National Jamboree. The activities were as thrilling as at previous jamborees: an opening ceremony with Vice President Richard M. Nixon in attendance . . . colorful pageants in the immense arena . . . historical hikes . . . campfires of friendship—and most thrilling of all, a closing ceremony during which the massed Scouts rededicated themselves to the Scout Oath in the flickering light from more than fifty thousand tiny candle flames.

For the Golden Jubilee Jamboree—the fifth in the series of national jamborees—the Scouts again travel to a western state. They will pitch their tents north of Colorado Springs, Colorado, with Pike's Peak looming over their campsite like a gigantic totem.

NATIONAL JAMBOREES

"YOU CAN'T KEEP a good man down." You can't keep a good thing within the borders of a single country.

Baden-Powell had hardly published the first installments of *Scouting for Boys* in the early days of 1908 before Scout troops and organizations began to spring up around the world—first within the British Empire, but immediately after in country after country.

In March, 1908, Scout troops were reporting to the Chief Scout from Cape Town, South Africa, and Sydney, Australia. Baden-Powell himself could announce, in October, 1908, that "the handbook has been translated into Russian and Norwegian."

A patrol of English Scouts toured Germany in the summer of 1909—in the fall, hundreds of German patrols had been formed. Baden-Powell visited South America in 1909, with the predictable result that Chile and Argentina decided to take up Scouting. Denmark also started Scouting in 1909. A Swedish army officer picked up a copy of *Scouting for Boys* in a ship's library on a Baltic journey, decided to translate it, and became Sweden's Chief Scout. Scouting came officially to Holland in 1910. In France, the *Eclaireurs de France* was formed in 1911. Switzerland joined the ranks the same year. By 1913 fifteen countries, including the United States, had their own organizations.

The Boy Scout movement had become a world brotherhood.

During World War I there were many dire predictions that Scouting would never survive the cataclysm. Instead of weakening, the Scout movement emerged from the war stronger than ever, with a greatly increased membership.

In 1920, in conjunction with the First World Jamboree, delegations of Chief Scouts and other national leaders from twenty-two countries met in London and determined to strengthen further the world aspect of Scouting. They decided that delegates from every country should meet every two years in an International Conference, that an International Committee should be formed to consider the needs of Scouting as one world movement, that an International Bureau should be established to keep all member countries informed on matters affecting World Scouting and to assist in the planning and organization of world jamborees.

Since then, Scouting has prospered and the ties of the world brotherhood have grown stronger and stronger. Today, more than eight million boys in sixty-seven countries call each other "Brother-Scouts."

United States of America

WORLD
SCOUTING

France

Greece

156

Australia

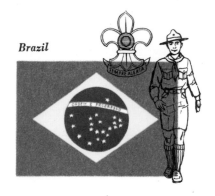

Brazil

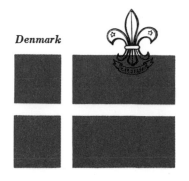

Denmark

Sudan

England

India

1. Argentina
2. Armenia
3. Australia
4. Austria
5. Belgium
6. Bolivia
7. Brazil
8. Burma
9. Canada
10. Ceylon

11. Chile
12. Colombia
13. Costa Rica
14. Cuba
15. Denmark
16. Dominican Republic
17. Ecuador
18. Egypt
19. El Salvador
20. Finland

21. France
22. Germany
23. Great Britain
24. Greece
25. Guatemala
26. Haiti
27. Iceland
28. India
29. Indonesia
30. Ireland

31. Israel
32. Italy
33. Japan
34. Korea
35. Lebanon
36. Liechtenstein
37. Luxembourg
38. Mexico
39. Netherlands
40. New Zealand

41. Nicaragua
42. Norway
43. Pakistan
44. Panama
45. Peru
46. Philippines
47. Portugal
48. South Africa
49. Sweden
50. Switzerland

51. Syria
52. Taiwan
53. Thailand
54. Turkey
55. United States of America
56. Uruguay
57. Venezuela

ALSO:
    Honduras
    Iran

Iraq
Jordan
Kuwait
Libya
Malayan Federation
Sudan
Tunisia
Viet-Nam

IT HAD BEEN Baden-Powell's hope to call the Boy Scouts of the world together in 1918 to celebrate the tenth anniversary of the public launching of the Boy Scout movement. But a war was raging—and celebrations had to wait. The dream remained—and in 1920 Scouts from twenty-one nations met in London for the first world "jamboree"—as Baden-Powell had insisted on calling it.

WORLD JAMBOREES

This first jamboree was an indoor affair held in Olympia—London's Madison Square Garden. It consisted of big displays for a large enthusiastic audience, and world competitions in Scoutcraft and in physical fitness skills. The most outstanding event of the jamboree occurred on the night of August 6, when Baden-Powell was acclaimed "Chief Scout of the World."

Four years later, the Boy Scouts of the world met for an entirely different kind of jamboree—an outdoor, camping jamboree—in a magnificent setting outside Copenhagen, Denmark. With its friendship emphasis and demonstrations of camp skills, it set the pattern for the jamborees that followed.

The "Coming-of-Age-Jamboree" in 1929 was logically laid in Scouting's homeland, England—at Arrowe Park, Birkenhead. In spite of the rain that turned the camp streets into mud, the spirit was high. It rose another few notches when the Prince of Wales announced to the assembled Scouts that his father, King George V, had honored Baden-Powell by raising him to the peerage. B.-P. had become Lord Baden-Powell of Gilwell.

The Boy Scouts of Hungary were the hosts for the fourth jamboree in 1933. It was held at the former royal hunting

England 1920

preserves at Gödöllö, near Budapest, and became a jamboree of music—the Hungarian troops had brought along gypsy bands and played and sang throughout the camping days.

To Holland in 1937 came Scouts from thirty-six different countries for a gathering of twenty-seven thousand at the fifth jamboree. This proved to be the last jamboree in which Baden-Powell took part. "His boys" surged around him as he gave them his closing message and his "God bless you all!"

Soon after, Baden-Powell left for Africa to spend the last years of his life in the land in which he had had so many adventures. The darkness of war spread over the world.

When the Scout movement had emerged from the war stronger than ever, the Boy Scouts of France invited their brother-Scouts to meet on French soil in 1947. The President of France himself opened this "Jamboree of Peace" at Moisson—half-way between Paris and Rouen.

After another interval of four years, Austria became the host country for the Seventh World Jamboree, held in a valley outside of Bad Ischl, a few miles from Salzburg. The campsite was the most beautiful of any jamboree location. It was surrounded by mountains that echoed with the campfire singing.

"The Jamboree of New Horizons" of 1955 met in Canada—at Niagara-on-the-Lake, Ontario. It was the first world jamboree outside Europe. The organization was splendid and the spirit of friendship as high as at any previous jamboree.

The "Jubilee Jamboree" in 1957, in Sutton Park, Birmingham, England, was called especially for the purpose of celebrating the one-hundredth anniversary of the birth of Baden-Powell and the fiftieth anniversary of the world's first Boy Scout camp on Brownsea Island. The main celebrations took the form of pageantry depicting the exciting events in the life of the Chief Scout of the World—with the present Lord Baden-Powell playing the part of his father.

Of all the Jamborees, number ten, in the Philippines in 1959, probably had a greater world aspect than any of the others. With the jamboree site almost half-way around the world from Europe and America, many participants used the occasion to circle the globe—as the Scout movement itself has done during the half-century of its existence.

Denmark 1924

Hungary 1933

Holland 1937

Philippines 1959

France 1947

SINCE ITS FOUNDING, men of national importance have been proud to be associated with Scouting. In 1910, Theodore Roosevelt accepted the title of Chief Scout Citizen. President William Howard Taft became the Honorary President. All succeeding presidents have served in this capacity.

Of the millions of men who have served Scouting, none have surpassed the nine presidents of the National Council. The first president, Colin H. Livingstone, serving from 1910 to 1924, contributed greatly to the formation of the basic policies that have made the movement strong.

James J. Storrow became Scouting's second president in May, 1925. He saw as Scouting's greatest need the strengthening of the training program and gave leadership to the establishment of the first national training school for Scout executives. His term of office ended with his untimely death in March of 1926.

Milton A. McRae, who had served as a charter member and vice president of the National Council from 1911 to 1924, became the third president in 1926, filling the balance of President Storrow's term.

Walter W. Head became Scouting's fourth president in May, 1926, and continued in that post for twenty years, except for a one month period in 1931. President Head guided the movement through the difficult years of the depression and of World War II. During this time he participated in Scouting activities in every state of the Union and in many foreign countries.

Mortimer L. Schiff, the fifth president, was a charter member of the National Executive Board. He had made numerous

far-reaching contributions to the organization and had served as International Commissioner to the world program. He died only a month after taking over the presidency.

Amory Houghton, United States ambassador to France during the Eisenhower administration, became the sixth president in 1946 and served until 1951. His presidency was marked by extensive program changes and promotional procedures that contributed to exceptional growth.

In 1951, John M. Schiff, son of Scouting's fifth president, became the seventh president of the National Council. During his administration, which ended in 1956, both the first nationwide "Get-Out-the-Vote" campaign and the National Conservation campaigns were conducted.

Kenneth K. Bechtel, first president to have been a Boy Scout, became the eighth president in 1956. He traveled extensively in the interests of Scouting. He placed emphasis on the need for adequate local organization and support to serve the expanding boy population and achieved significant results. The new Exploring program was launched.

Ellsworth H. Augustus was elected in June, 1959. He is a well-prepared Scouter, having served as council president, regional chairman, and on the National Executive Board.

The presidents of the Boy Scouts of America have truly been "top volunteers." They have always faced their task as a challenge and an adventure and have never considered their service as a sacrifice made. They have always faced the future with vision and courage. They have truly led the way.

The Goal Ahead

By ARTHUR A. SCHUCK
Chief Scout Executive

THE RECORD OF THE PAST has been written. But no movement can rest on its past—the very word "movement" suggests progression.

The task of the Boy Scouts of America in the days that lie ahead presents a tremendous challenge and at the same time great opportunities. Words are of little value unless they are backed by dedicated, constructive action. The enrollment of over 1,250,000 volunteer adults in Scouting becomes truly significant only in direct proportion to the earnest and active participation of those who volunteer.

The development of our youth to be physically strong, mentally awake, and morally straight—to be citizens of character, with high spiritual ideals and motives—is not just a desirable thing; it is essential if America is to fulfill its mission as the leader of the Free World.

To this end, Scouting is preparing the boys of our country for vital participation as men in the affairs of the nation and of the world. Because we have confidence in the Boy Scouts of America and its contribution to physical fitness, character building, and citizenship training, we must go forward with it aggressively.

As we do so, we must keep in mind that tremendous parade of youth growing up in the years before us, and safeguard the future of our country by adequately training our boys in those things that make for the spiritually minded, dedicated citizen who will, in turn, guarantee the future freedom not only of America but of the world.

This is the goal to which the Boy Scouts of America stands dedicated.

INDEX

Advancement and Special Events Service, 133
Advancement, Boy Scout, 74–82
Advancement, Cub Scout, 48
Advisor, Explorer, 117
Aids to Scouting, 22
Air Scouting, 42
Akela, 46, 48
Alexander, John L., 26, 126
American Boy Scout, 25, 26
Arrow Points, 62
Assistant Chief Scout Executive, 132
Assistant to Chief Scout Executive, 132

Baden-Powell, Lady, 23
Baden-Powell, Lord, 10, 14, 15, 16–23, 34, 35, 36, 39, 40, 41, 44, 115, 118, 125, 144, 154
Baden-Powell, Warington, 91
Badges of Merit, 41
Bear Cub Scout, 60, 62
Beard, Daniel Carter, 26, 27, 40, 118
Berryman, Clifford H., 40
"Black Book," 136
Bobcat, 60
Boer War, 20
Bomus, Peter S., 26
Boyce, William D., 14, 24
Boy Scout *Handbook*, 144–47, 150
"Boy Scout Scheme," 22, 115
Boy Scouting, 66–89
Boy Scouting Service, 132
Boy Scouts of America, founding, 14
Boy Scouts of United States, 25, 26
Boys' Brigade, 22
Boys' Life, 132, 137, 148–49
Brownsea Island, 22

Campfires, 83
Camping Service, 133
Camping, Scout, 140
Camporee, 84
Campsites, local, 143
Campsites, national, 143
Carey, Arthur A., 91
Catholic Committee, 123
Catholic Service, 133
Central Typing Service, 133
Charterhouse School, 16
Chief Scout, 26, 27, 31
Chief Scout Executive, 30, 32, 33, 132
"Chief Scout of the World," 23
Chief Seascout, 93

Children's Bureau, 30
Church of Jesus Christ of Latter-day Saints, 124
Churchill, Winston, 46
Citizenship Experiences, 112
"Citizens Now" Conferences, 113
Civic Relationships Service, 133
Columbia University, 32, 41
Committee on Badges, Awards, 35, 40
Committee on Finance, 35, 42
Committee on Organization, 35, 42
Committee on Standardization, 35
Consultant, Explorer, 96
Cruising for Sea Scouts, 91
Cubbing, 42
Cubmaster, 46, 48, 54, 55, 118, 119
Cub Scout, 42, 66
Cub Scout Achievements, 59, 60
Cub Scout Badges, 48, 60, 64
Cub Scout Books, 144
Cub Scout Handshake, 51
Cub Scout Motto, 51
Cub Scout Promise, 50
Cub Scout Salute, 51
Cub Scout Sign, 48, 51
Cub Scout Uniform, 63
Cub Scouting, 44–65, 119
Cub Scouting Service, 132

Den, 49, 51, 53
Den Chief, 49, 53, 54, 119
Den Mother, 48, 53, 54, 118, 119
Deputy Chief Scout Executive, 132
Districts, 127
Divisional Plan, 132

Eagle Scout, 41, 87
Editorial Board, 42
Editorial Service, 133
Education Division, 133
Eisenhower, Dwight D., 155, 160
Engineering Service, 133
Executive Board, 129
Explorer Advisor, 117, 123
Explorer Code, 98
Explorer Emblem, 99
Explorer Motto, 98
Explorer Salute, 98
Explorer Uniform, 99
Exploring, 42, 95–113, 119
Exploring Program, 97
Exploring Service, 132

Federal Charter, 67, 123
Field Department, 32
Field Operations, 132
Finance Service, 132
First Class Scout, 39, 80–82
Fisher, George J., 126
Fretwell, Elbert K., 32

"Get-Out-the-Vote" campaigns, 153
Gilwell Park, 15
Gold Honor Medal, 89, 150
Good Turn Idea, 150
Good Turns, national, 33, 153
Grant, Gordon, 146

Handbook for Boys, 42, 123, 144–47

Handbook for Patrol Leaders, 119
Handbook for Scoutmasters, 70, 113, 118, 122
Handbooks, 144
Handicapped Scouts, 139
Headquarters Gazette, 44, 117
Health and Safety Service, 133
Historical Museum, 137
Home in Cub Scouting, 48, 50
Hornaday Award, 88
Houghton, Alanson Bigelow, 15
Hurt, H. W., 47

Indian Scouts, 139
Institutional Representative, 126
International Bureau, 156
International Committee, 156
International Conference, 156
International Service, 133
Interracial Service, 133

Jagger, David, 11
Jamborees, national, 33, 84, 156
Jamborees, world, 23, 33, 84, 158
Jenks, Jeremiah W., 36
Jewish Committee, 124
Jewish Service, 133
Johnston, Gale F., 137
Jungle Books, The, 45

Kelly, Colin P., Jr., 160
Kelly, Colin P., III, 160
Kipling, Rudyard, 45

Lane, Joseph, 148
Law of the Pack, 50
Lawrence, Ernest O., 161
Leadership, Boy Scouting, 116–18
Leadership, Cub Scouting, 48, 119
Leadership, Exploring, 96, 119
Leyendecker, J. C., 146
Life Scout, 41, 87
Lion Cub Scout, 60, 63
Livingstone, Colin H., 26
Local Council, 124–27

Mafeking, 20–21
McKenzie, R. Tait, 137
Medal of Merit, 89, 150
Membership, 138
Merit Badge Counselor, 117
Merit Badge Program, 86
Merit badges, 41, 86
Meyer, G. V. L., 92
Mormon Service, 133
Mowgli, 45
Museum, Historical, 137

National Council, 129
National Court of Honor, 89, 150
National Office, 30, 136
National Scouts of America, 25, 26
National Scout Commissioner, 26, 27
National Service, 153
National Staff, 130–35
Negro Scouts, 139
New Brunswick, N.J., 136

Officers, National, 128
Operations Division, 32
Organization, local, 121–27
Organization, national, 128–35
Outdoor Experiences, 106

Pack, 49, 51
Pack Committee, 123
Pack, Law of, 50
Pack, Life in, 54
Pack meeting, 54
Pack Theme, 56
Patrol, 67, 68
Patrol Leader, 68, 119
Peace Scouts of California, 25
Personal Fitness Experiences, 108
Personnel Division, 133
Phillips, Waite, 143
Philmont, 133, 143
Philtower, 133
Post, 96
Post activities, 100
Post Specialties, 101
Post Super-activities, 100
Program Division, 132
Program Resources Service, 133
Parents in Cub Scouting, 54
Presbrey, Frank, 149
Protestant Committee, 123
Protestant Service, 133
Printing and Production Service, 133
Public Relations Service, 133

Regions, 135
Relationships Division, 133
Religious Awards, 88
Research Service, 133
Robinson, Edgar M., 24, 25, 118, 125
Rockefeller Memorial Foundation, 47, 95
Rockwell, Norman, 7, 37, 43, 52, 65, 85, 95, 114, 142, 147, 149, 151
Roosevelt, Franklin Delano, 154, 160, 161
Roosevelt, Theodore, 26, 30
Rural Service, 133
Russell, James E., 41

Saint Nicholas Magazine, 45
Schiff, Mortimer L., 143
Schiff, Mrs. Jacob, 143
Schiff Scout Reservation, 133, 143
School Service, 133
Schuck, Arthur A., 32–33, 162
Scout Badge, 40
Scout Commissioner, 126
Scout Commissioner, National, 26, 27
Scout Executive, 126
Scout Field Book, 144
Scout Handshake, 73
Scout Law, 35, 36, 38, 72
Scout Motto, 72
Scout Oath, 35, 36, 38, 72
Scout-o-rama, 84
Scout Requirements, 39
Scout Sign, 73
Scout Slogan, 72
Scout Uniform, 40, 73
Scouter's Key, 115
Scouting for Boys, 22, 24, 34, 41, 90, 144, 156
Scouting for older boys, 90–113
Scouting Magazine, 117, 137
Scoutmaster, 70, 116, 119, 122
Sea Scouting, 42, 90, 91

Sea Scouting for Boys, 91
Seascout Manual, 93
Second Class Scout, 39, 76–79
Senior Scouting, 95
Service Clubs, 124
Service Experiences, 110
Seton, Ernest Thompson, 25, 118, 145
Silver Buffalo, 15
Silver Wolf, 41
Smith, Sir William, 22
Smyth, Sir Henry, 20
Social Experiences, 104
Sons of Daniel Boone, 25, 27
Spear, Mrs. Ellis, 28
Sponsoring Institutions, 123
Star Scout, 41, 87
Statistical Service, 133
"Strengthen the Arm of Liberty," 32
Subscription Fulfillment Service, 133
Supply Service Division, 132

Taft, William Howard, 26, 161
Tenderfoot Scout, 39, 64, 74–75
Troop, 67, 70
Troop Committee, 121, 122

Truman, Harry S., 154
University of Michigan, 95
Unknown Scout, 13, 15
Verbeck, William, 26
Visual Education Service, 133
Vocational Experiences, 102
Volunteer Leaders, 115–19
Volunteer Training Service, 118

Webelos, 64
Webelos Den, 64
West, James Edward, 26, 28–31, 32, 35, 38, 92, 117, 118, 119, 126, 132, 145
White House Conference, 30
Wilder, James Austin, 92
Wilson, Woodrow, 67
Wolf Cub, 45
Wolf Cub's Handbook, The, 46
Wolf Cub Scout, 60, 62
Wolf Cub Scout Book, 48
Woodcraft Indians, 25, 27
World Chief Guide, 23
World Friendship Fund, 33
World Scouting, 156–57
World War I, 92, 152, 156
World War II, 95, 152
YMCA, 24, 25

BIBLIOGRAPHY

Books published by Boy Scouts of America unless otherwise indicated.

GENERAL HISTORY

The Piper of Pax, by E. K. Wade. C. Arthur Pearson Ltd., London, 1931
Baden-Powell, by E. E. Reynolds. Oxford University Press, London, 1957
Twenty-One Years of Scouting, by E. K. Wade. C. Arthur Pearson Ltd., London, 1929
History of the Boy Scouts of America, by William D. Murray. 1937
Annual Reports, Boy Scouts of America. 1911–current
SCOUTING Magazine. 1913–current

CUB SCOUTING

The Wolf-Cub's Handbook, by Sir Robert S. S. Baden-Powell. C. Arthur Pearson Ltd., London, 1916
The Boy's Cubbooks: I Wolf Rank, II Bear Rank, III Lion Rank, edited by H. W. Hurt. 1930–31
Wolf Cub Scout Book, Bear Cub Scout Book, Lion Cub Scout Book, by Gerald A. Speedy. 1948
Cubmaster's Pack Book, edited by Gerald A. Speedy. 1954

BOY SCOUTING

Scouting for Boys, by Sir Robert S. S. Baden-Powell. C. Arthur Pearson Ltd., London, 1908
Boy Scouts of America, Official Handbook, by Ernest Thompson Seton and Sir Robert S. S. Baden-Powell. Doubleday, Page & Co., New York, 1910
Handbook for Boys, developed by Editorial Board, B. S. A. Doubleday, Page & Co., New York, 1911
Boy Scout Handbook, by William Hillcourt. 1959
Aids to Scoutmastership, by Sir Robert S. S. Baden-Powell. Herbert Jenkins Ltd., London, 1920
Handbook for Scoutmasters, developed by Editorial Board, B. S. A. 1913
Handbook for Scoutmasters, by William Hillcourt. 1936–37

EXPLORING

Cruising for Sea Scouts, by Arthur A. Carey. Privately printed, 1913
Nautical Scouting, compiled by Charles Longstretch. 1915
The Seascout Manual, edited by James A. Wilder. 1920
Adventuring for Senior Scouts, edited by H. W. Hurt. 1938
Air Scout Manual, edited by H. W. Hurt. 1942
Exploring, by Ted S. Holstein. 1958

ON MY HONOR I

+ TO DO MY DUTY

COUNTRY AND TO

LAW   + TO HELP

ALL TIMES   + TO

PHYSICALLY STRO

AWAKE AND MO